An Insignificant Life?

A True Story of a Life Stolen by a Dirty
District Attorney and a Corrupt Police
Department

Ira Leon

Printed in the United States of America by
BestSelf Publications
bestselfpublications@gmail.com
bestselfpublications.com

First and foremost, all thanks be to my Lord and God.

To my mother, Martha Leon-Pruitt, and to all those innocent of the crimes they are incarcerated for due to the illegal and immoral actions of unworthy civil servant

Editor's Note

One week before I ever met Ira, my girlfriend wished that I had an older gentleman in my life who was a prisoner like myself, who has been down much longer than me.... someone who knows what it's like. She wished for someone I could relate to because they alone understand what I'm going through coping year after year with a life sentence for a murder I didn't commit - because I had no one.

Yes, there have always been "older lifers" around me who have spent all their life in prison, but none of Ira's caliber - who have kept their sanity throughout all the years, let alone their morals. Someone who could be a good person while still standing on principle. I needed to see that it was possible, that I wasn't the only one struggling in my fight for justice, that there were older guys who have been through what I'm going through - without coming out on the other end completely shattered.

My girlfriend said it out loud, she spoke her desire into the universe... and I kid you not, one week later Ira was moved into the group of inmates whom I'm allowed to interact with for 3 hours a day.

After being introduced to Ira and hearing his story, I knew that God had bumped him in my direction, answering my girlfriend's prayer. Like myself, Ira is serving a life sentence under the "felony murder" doctrine and has been incarcerated since he was 19-years old. If anyone could understand what it feels like, Ira does.

His story is heart shattering. An innocent man having served 33-years in prison for a crime he didn't commit... I mean, who couldn't feel for him? But Ira is more than that, he is More Than an Inmate.... he is humane, and his words express the gentle, caring soul that he is.

I am honored to be able to help share this story with the world. It is one you will not soon forget… one that may change your view of the justice system... but for sure a story that will touch your heart.

God has bumped this story into your hands for a reason... recognize that by listening to his words with compassion and acting upon what you believe to be righteous.

Be at home.

Thank you for your time

-Nicholas J. Ely
Author of "The Prisoner Manifesto"
www.morethananinmate.com
Facebook: More Than An Inmate
Tik Tok: @freenicholaesly
October 14th 2024

An Insignificant Life?

Prologue

In five short months I will have been incarcerated for 33 years. I sit here in this small cell wondering, hoping, praying for the day when this so-called "Justice for all U.S. citizens" will finally include me. I am a poor minority in this world who couldn't afford the luxury of a paid private attorney to represent me for a crime that I had no part in committing.

My name is Ira. I am a man who is innocent of murder but have been serving a life sentence for it since 1992. I have never stopped fighting in court for freedom. However, it is a very daunting, if not overwhelming, endeavour to navigate the legal system when you've had no formal training or education on how to do so. I found myself quickly in over my head fighting for my life but I will never stop.

Seventeen years after my sentencing, I caught a break in my case and thought I was finally headed home. I thought I had finally received the evidence that would prove my innocence and set me free. This evidence was a set of transcripts that included two witness statements that I had never seen before or even knew existed, and these statements shed light upon the truth. They were mailed to me by the state during one of the many court filings challenging my conviction.

You see, after I had just turned 19 years old, I was backed into a corner by an archaic "felony murder" law that D.A.'s weaponize to force pleas from co-defendants, or those down right innocent of any crime at all, as I was. Let me explain...

"Felony murder" is a murder that happened during the commission of an underlying felony (such as rape, robbery, burglary, kidnapping, arson, etc.). When a murder occurs during the act of one of these felonies, such as robbery, it does not matter who actually committed the murder because the "felony murder rule" finds anyone who is guilty of the underlying felony responsible for the murder itself... even if they had no part in it or intention to kill.

I was being charged with robbery so, because of the "felony murder rule", the burden of proof to find me guilty of murder is only proving that this robbery was committed and I had a part in it.

As I'm innocent of this crime and had no knowledge of it, for many years I believed that the store was robbed that day. I mean, the police and the store owner both stated the register was open and that all of the day's money was missing. If they said a robbery had taken place because the money was missing, why would I not believe them?

I've never known what actually happened in the store that day – whether a robbery took place or not - because I'm innocent of this crime. Proving that a robbery occurred was the only way the state could find me guilty of a murder they know I didn't commit.

Back to the two witness statements I discovered within the transcripts sent to me by the District Court Clerk....

After the crime scene was investigated and the evidence collected, the detectives turned over the store so they could clean up and get the store back in order for business again. The employee on shift at this time, Mrs. Diane Sivits, actually finds the "missing money" (that was claimed to have been stolen) inside of a candy box in neat stacks of ones, fives, tens and twenties - along with checks endorsed/signed by the deceased clerk.

Diane Sivits calls over the manager to show her the money and both were stumped. All three of these ladies (the manager, Mrs. Sivits, and the deceased clerk) had worked there for years and they all knew the combination to the safe. It's not part of their protocol to keep money in candy boxes "tilted on their side and pushed all the way back onto the shelf under the register." The manager and Mrs. Sivits wanted to know why it was there and how the police investigators missed it, so the manager called the owner.

To Mrs. Sivits surprise, the owner told the manager to put the money in her purse and said he would meet with her later to collect it. Mrs. Sivits spoke her displeasure of these actions to the owner but he tried to convince the two ladies to forget all about this because "they have all they need to get those boys."

Mrs. Sivits waited for the owner to come in the next day to confront him about this because she believed it's not right for anyone to be charged with a robbery when there wasn't a robbery. The owner again tried to persuade Mrs. Sivits to forget all about this, but she couldn't. She wouldn't. It weighed on her conscience. So, Mrs. Sivits went straight to the police station and demanded that her statement be taken. Officer Monte Vlasin took her statement and wrote one of his own. **<u>These statements were never handed over to me or my counsel until 17 years later!</u>**

These statements provided proof that no robbery had ever occurred. Since no robbery ever occurred, the "felony murder rule" no longer applied and I could not be held accountable for a murder that they know I didn't commit.

These are the witness statements I believed would finally send me home... but excitement was short-lived.

16 years later, I am still here...

This is my story.

October 2024

Chapter 1

It's February 17th, 1992, and this is my second day on the Greyhound bus from Sacramento, CA to North Platte, NE where my oldest brother, Raymond, had lived with his wife and three stepdaughters. I hadn't seen my brother in nearly 8 years so I had planned to come stay with him for at least a year. I was picked up by his wife, Jenny, at the bus station a little after noon. I came with all that I owned at the time - clothes, shoes, a little over $200, and an ounce of marijuana.

Once we got to the house, I met my three step nieces who were awesome. My brother was sleeping on the couch. My sister-in-law told me he worked the night shift at the beef plant in Lexington and would be asleep for a few hours. She showed me to the room I would be sleeping in and where I could unpack my belongings.

On the way to the room, I noticed two people sleeping in a bed next to the open door of the adjacent room. I put away some of my things and returned to the living room to ask Jenny who those people were in the other room. She told me it was a "young man"* the same age as myself (19) who my brother had met in town and his 28-year-old girlfriend, Karen. She told me how the young man had been staying with them for about three months and how the previous weekend he had met Karen at a bar in Lexington. Since then, she'd been staying there as well.

I started asking Jenny about possible job openings in town when Karen, now awake, came into the living room to join us. We were briefly introduced and the three of us continued talking about a variety of things, mostly about how Karen had always wanted to experience life in California. She was very inquisitive about how my life had been back home.

Eventually I turned the conversation back to how I was anxious to get out there and start putting in job applications. The girls said they'd convince the young man to let them use his car to take me around town. I asked them, "where does he work? Maybe he can help get me on with his employer?" but they both looked at each other and Karen said, "he doesn't have a job."

     *Note: Throughout my story, I refer to this 19-year-old as "young man" because he was and still is a stranger to me and I want to make that point clear. I did not and still do not know him, he is not my friend, and I had no association with him beyond this time. I have no intention or desire to ever speaking his name again. *

     So, back to the story, Jenny went on to tell me how the young man hadn't had a job before he started staying with them and hasn't even attempted to look for one. Karen then tells me how she had had two jobs and shared a five-bedroom home with a girlfriend of hers in Lexington but lost her jobs because the young man wanted her to stay in North Platte with him.

     After hearing about all of this, I began to feel like this young man was some freeloader who was taking advantage of my brother's hospitality. I went into the room and woke him up by introducing myself as Raymond's little brother, saying that he should get up and get ready so he could go out with us to put in job applications around town. I let him know that a job is a must or this isn't the place for him.

Within the hour we were all in his car driving around town filling out job applications for every business that was open at the time. Running low on gas, and because I was the only person in the vehicle with any money, Karen asked me if I would be willing to fill the tank and buy a case of beer to take a trip to Lexington so she could pick up her last pay checks as well as retrieve her half of the deposit on the house she shared with her girlfriend. She said if I did this, she'd pay for the same on the trip back, plus she'd cook me a steak and baked potato when we returned. How could I refuse that offer?

Chapter 2

The young man was driving. It was a two-door vehicle. Karen was in the passenger seat; I was sitting in the back behind the driver and my sister-in-law was next to me. We drank and smoked weed all the way to Lexington.

Once there, we went to Karen's first job and she was in and out. She said to go to her old place next so she could get her deposit check back and then they could go to her second job at a bar after which would allow her to cash all of the checks there. We all went in to meet her girlfriend and we stayed for awhile so we could smoke some weed with her. She was really nice and had lots to say about Karen leaving her life behind to live in North Platte. She made no qualm about voicing her concerns over the young man's lack of work, money or place to stay.

We left and drove over to the bar she worked at next. As she went in to take care of things, we all got out of the car and just stood around. I went to the side of the building to use the restroom before we hit the road again. As I came back around the building, Karen had come out with a case of Budweiser and a six-pack of Michelob (which she stated to all of us was for her only because this is the brand of beer she likes). I got back into the car behind the driver's seat while Karen was whispering to Jenny. Then Jenny asked the young man if she could drive back. He said no problem but while this verbal exchange was happening, Karen ran around to the passenger side of the car to get into the back seat with me. He stood there just looking at her until she said "get in, let's get going."

There was this build up with the two of us since I had arrived, just a feeling inside, but she began making things clear to all of us exactly how she was feeling as the day progressed. We stopped at a gas station to fill up the tank and the young man tried to get Karen to sit up front with Jenny but she wouldn't get out and just kept telling him to stop making such a big deal about things.

Once back on the road he continued turning in his seat to pick at her and one of the things he chose to pester her about was a little brown paper bag she had brought out with the beer from the bar. She kept telling him it was none of his business what she had in the bag. It was hers and it was not for him. Jenny turned on the music and asked me to roll a couple joints to pass around. This forced the young man to settle back and leave her alone.

Karen and I started talking and, almost as if to antagonize the young man, she picked up the little brown bag out of her lap and asked me to guess what was inside. This drew an immediate response from him and he demanded to know what was in "the fucking bag." She just blew him off, telling him it's none of his business and has nothing to do with him.

Her and I continued talking and I finished my beer so I could roll another joint. She grabbed the empty can and tossed it out of the passenger window, then quickly slid one of her Michelob's out for me to try the brand she likes. At this point I was confident that Karen's fling with the young man was done and she was pushing for her and I to hook-up.

As the marijuana joint was being passed around the car, and Karen was fussing over me now. I took the last drink from my beer when we were turning off the highway into North Platte. Karen grabbed the empty bottle from me to throw out the window but first had to ask the young man to roll the window back down. By this point he was fuming and was on her about why she was doing so much for me. She told him, "I'm just throwing out the bottle because I'm on the side next to the edge of the road so roll down the damn window!" She was so frustrated and distracted with the back-and-forth bickering that when he finally rolled the window down, she accidently threw out the little brown paper bag with the bottle! She didn't even blink before she was yelling to Jenny to stop the car.

Jenny pulled over to the side of the road and Karen was pushing the seat forward telling him to open the door. Jenny was telling her she'd back up but as soon as he opened the door, Karen was out like a shot running back for that little brown paper bag!

Jenny backed up the car and Karen met them on her way back. She got in all happy and laughing, saying "I got it!"

Now the young man was furious, demanding to know what's so important about that little brown paper bag. She again told him that it's none of his business, that it's not for him, and then focused her attention back to me. She was giggling and asking if I wanted to know what was in her little brown paper bag. By this point I'm sure everyone wanted to know what Karen was hiding so of course I said yes! She opened it up and pulled out... some packages of Pop Rock candy. Dumbfounded, I waited for the rest but she only pulled out more packets of candy. I was oblivious until Jenny blurts out that Pop Rocks are used to make a game out of a few sex acts.

That was the moment it became clear to everyone in the car that Karen was no longer interested in pursuing her fling with the young man. She was clearly choosing to pursue me but had yet to verbalize the actual "break up" to the young man.

Chapter 3

I lay out all of these events for the reader to express the domestic tension in the atmosphere at the time, the dynamics between myself and the young man, and the reasons for which he was fuming with jealousy and anger. Of course, the alcohol hadn't helped matters much.

Now back at the house... the two of them are in a full-fledged shouting match. He's screaming at her about all the attention she's showing me and she's yelling back how I had just gotten here, and, not only was I out looking for a job but had to get on him to start looking for one as well. Karen finally had had enough and asked Jenny to take her to the store so they could get some things for dinner.

All smiles, Karen came into the living room to tell me they were going shopping and how she was going to cook me up the best steak with baked potato that I'd ever had, just like she'd promised.

When they left to the store, I just chilled on the couch under the noisy air conditioner that my brother was sleeping on earlier. I rolled a joint to smoke and just watched the young man pace around until he finally sat in an armchair on the other side of the living room. I didn't speak to him, nor did I offer him anything.

It was just the two of us left in the house. My brother had caught his ride to work earlier while we were on our trip to Lexington. Jenny had taken her daughters to stay with their grandmother earlier that morning. So, we sat in the living room alone, not speaking to each other, in silence until Jenny and Karen came back from the store. Sitting in silence was more than okay with me because I had already formulated a bad opinion of this guy. No job, scruffy looking, acted like a child, had no goals, no desires, and no initiative to obtain something better for himself. Looking back now, he probably had mental health problems that nobody realized at the time.

There was nothing between us but the sounds from the noisy air conditioner until the girls returned. Karen and Jenny went straight to the kitchen to begin cooking and the young man was back in action. Full throttle! He's in the kitchen now, harassing Karen about who she's cooking for. Karen tells him how she's cooking for her and I, and that Jenny was making something else for him. But not steak.

With that, the screaming and yelling quickly began. The whole time I'm just patiently waiting for Karen to voice her intentions outright, to stop beating around the bush. He wasn't catching all the indicators that everyone else had picked up on a long time ago. Karen wanted nothing more to do with the young man but he wasn't accepting it. Instead, he began to spiral into his emotions.

Karen brought my meal out to me and… heck yes it was pretty good! She even did up the baked potato with shredded cheese, sour cream, and bacon bits. I asked her to come eat with me but she said she needed to figure things out because "he's just not getting it."

I told her she might be able to figure it out if she simply told him outright, and then said to let me know if she needed my help with anything.

The domestic argument between the two retired behind closed doors in the bedroom.

After I finished eating, I went in the kitchen to wash my dishes. Jenny was there being nosey, trying to make out what was being said between Karen and the young man. Jenny said this was all my fault because Karen wants to get with me.

I noticed Karen's uneaten plate on the table and looked questioningly at Jenny. She said he wouldn't give her any time to eat it.

She filled me in on some their discussion she'd overheard. Apparently, he was trying to get Karen to give him money so he could buy some cocaine. He was telling her that he knows she wants to sleep with me now and he doesn't care because he wants to get back together with his ex-girlfriend anyways.

Karen came out of the room and sat in the kitchen saying she doesn't care what he does but she's not giving him any money. She picked at her plate but I could see she really wanted to just have girl-to-girl talk so

I told them I was going to kick back in the living room.

It couldn't have been ten minutes later when he came rolling out of the bedroom with a full head of steam and went straight into the kitchen to pick up where he'd left off. They were really going at it - and I mean going at it - and I mean top volume! This went on for fifteen or more minutes with Jenny running back and forth from them in the kitchen, to me in the living room. She kept telling me to do something. I told her to stay out of it, that she's dumping him but he's playing stupid because she hasn't outright said so yet. But Jenny wouldn't stop; she was amping herself up to solve a problem that was none of her business.

I finally got tired of Jenny asking me to intervene so I yelled into the kitchen and demanded that all parties to shut the hell up! I said, "Look. We were having a great day partying together so let's just take a breather from this b.s." I suggested we give Jenny some money to take the young man to buy some beer since we'd finished off all we had.

This interruption at least got the fighting to stop but I could still hear him asking Karen for money to buy cocaine. She stayed firm on the "no, it's not going to happen" response.

That was good but now Jenny was back in the living room bothering me again because she decided she didn't want to go with the young man to buy the beer. She said I should go. "No, no no" was my immediate answer. I explained that I didn't like this whiney dude and that I was trying to get some time alone with Karen.

Jenny refused to go, but I was just as adamant about not going either... the dude could go by himself. He doesn't need someone to go with him.

Now the young man himself didn't even want to go and was back trying to start an argument with Kalen again. Jenny begins crying around, saying that I need to get him out of the house for awhile. No way was I planning on going anywhere with this guy, I didn't even know him!

I argued with Jenny, telling her "you wanted me to get involved so I did and got him to back off Karen, and I got him to go with you to the store to buy more beer. Now you want to stay behind and send me off with him when you know that Karen and I are trying to spend time together?! You know this guy. I don't. Why would I go with him?!?"

Jenny then leaves me to go talk with Karen and, after a couple of minutes, Karen comes in the room to ask me to please go with him so she can get some space away from him. She assured me not to worry because we'd talk later. She informed me she'd broken up with him, and that he's swearing he's going to get back with his ex-girlfriend.

I let Karen convince me to go with him. I told her I'd go buy some more beer and get this guy out of the house for a little bit to blow off some steam. We'd be back soon.

Chapter 4

I don't know what time it was but it had been dark out for awhile before we thought about getting some beer again. I'm in the car with him now, headed to the store, when he starts questioning me about things my brother Raymond had told him about me and my other brother, Raul. "Was this true? Is that true? Did this really happen? Did your other brother really just get out of prison for a murder when he was younger?"

I didn't like that my brother Ray had shared so much personal family history with this guy so I just kept pushing the conversation back to him. "Was he born here? Did he ever have a job? Why can't he stay with his own family?" Small talk.

He told me he couldn't get along with his stepdad and that his mom always took her new husband's side on everything. Then he started telling me about this girl, April, who he used to go out with. They had been going out for a long time, they were the love of each other's lives but had gotten into a fight a few weeks prior and split up. He explained to me that that's when he was partying up in Lexington and had met Karen.

By this time, he had pulled into the parking lot of the second store we'd gone to so far but, just like with the first store, he drove past the front to look at the clerk on shift, stated for the second time that this clerk wouldn't sell them alcohol without an I.D. either. We were both only 19 so neither of us could legally purchase alcohol from anywhere.

So, he eased back into traffic as he said there's a store near where April lived that would sell to us. We drove around for another 15-20 minutes as he moaned about how much he loved and missed April. Talking about her and their relationship had brought him to tears, making him very emotional. Granted, we had been drinking and smoking all day.

I wasn't in the mood for all this, all I wanted to do was head back to the house. For the third time I told him to either "take me to a damn store or drop me back off at the house because I didn't sign on for a trip around town."

He drove into a more residential neighborhood and then pulled into an alley where he then parked. I asked him "what the heck is going on? This isn't a store and this isn't the house?" He opened his door and got out as he said "April's house is on the block over. At the end of her street is a dead end but there's a store on the other side." He asked me if I would go to April's house with him first so he could see if he could get her to come out and talk to him. Then, we'd go get the beer.

Fed up of him and wanting to get this over with as quickly as possible, I didn't argue and told him "Let's go" as I got out of the car. I started walking towards her house but turned around when he called me back. He was at the trunk of the car with it open but he closed the trunk before I got to him or could see inside. He had a crowbar in one hand and tried to hand me a tire iron. I asked him why the hell we would need those, to which he said he was scared of April's dad because her dad didn't like him and had gotten physical with him before.

I told him, "I don't need a weapon. For one, this isn't my business. And secondly, I can physically hold my own in an altercation." I told him to put those things back and I started walking towards the street where I saw a parked boat next to some cars in the driveway and the next street ahead. He caught up and put the crowbar under the boat but still had the tire iron. I told him to get rid of that too so he went behind the boat. When he returned, the tire iron was gone.

With him now leading the way, we started up the street. He pointed to the dead end up the block and said "there's a hole in the fence and right over the train tracks is the store." Then he pointed to a house still a little way up the street and claimed it was April's house.

When we arrived at the house, we stopped and I looked at him. Then I looked at the house. It was pretty dark and there wasn't a light on in or even around the house. It was all black.

After standing there for a moment I told him to go over there and get her attention. I asked if he could get to her bedroom window but he said that he doesn't want to go over there now because he's scared of waking up her dad, suggesting maybe he should just try to call her.

All of this nonsense had me pretty pissed off. This dude was wasting my time dragging me to do all of this with him, just for him to chicken out right in front of her house. Especially after all that damn crying he did about her!

Annoyed, I told him to show me to the store so we could get back to my brother's house. After looking over the dark house and giving up on getting April's attention, he took the lead and walked the few feet left to the dead end. He showed me the hole in the fence and climbed through it up and over the train tracks and, just like he said, was the parking lot of a store. He kept walking and I followed across the lot. Finally, we were about to buy some beer and I could get back home to Karen.

Chapter 5

I was walking a little behind him, really just lost in my own thoughts about how I was going to handle this situation with Karen. I mean, she was older than me but was really a good-looking woman. We had a connection, for sure, and she was a hard worker who wanted something more out of life.

Thoughts of Karen consumed me until we were almost to the front doors of the store. The whole front of the building was windows. I was looking through the windows at the tables and counters inside, just amazed at how that part of the store was like a cafeteria. The young man entered the building with me on his heels.

The first thing I noticed was how I didn't hear any beep or bells upon entry. In

California, stores were like bank vaults; you couldn't enter without a clerk being notified.

I looked at the coolers and seen the beer. There was a lady between the two coolers that ran the length of the store. I'm not even three steps into the store as I took all of this in. And I never took another step further into that store...

(Editor's Note: At this point, Ira has made the decision to leave out details of what he witnessed because the purpose of his story was not to detail the crime itself. Ira is innocent of felony murder and was wrongfully convicted of all charges. Continue reading for an explanation by Ira as to why he has decided to leave the actual crime out of this story.)

I ran out the door and sprinted back to the car.

Minutes were going by as I sat in the passenger seat waiting for this dude, so I got out and walked back to the mouth of the alley. I didn't see him, so I walked the half block to the street light on the corner to look down the street with the dead end. I didn't see anything for a minute, then I finally seen a shape walking out of the dark towards me. I noticed it was him as he walked back to the car and got in.

As soon as he got in next to me, I told him to take me the fuck back home! He didn't say a word. We were driving through residential areas for awhile in silence. I tried to look at him but his long uncut rocker hair completely covered his face, so I asked him, "What the fuck?!" He never uttered a single word so I just watched as we drove from one street to the next until we turned into an alley and I seen the back door to the house. We were finally home.

I walked into the house through the back door. My mind was in overdrive with every possible thought of how this could affect me, or if it would. Walking up the hallway that led into the living room, my sister-in-law Jenny came running at me out of the kitchen yelling, "Was it you?! Was it you that killed that store clerk?!" I was stunned! This is how I first heard what had actually happened. I stood there for a moment in disbelief. The young man walked by me and sat down in the armchair. I asked Jenny what she was talking about - she said someone robbed the Bain Store and killed the clerk. I couldn't believe it.

I noticed other people now. There were 7 or 8 people in the house and all of them began grabbing up purses and coats and heading out the door. Jenny was telling me that her mom had called to inform her there was a robbery/murder at the Bain Store. She said that her mom sits at home monitoring the police scanners all day. She said her mom had asked where I was because the description of the suspect matched me. All this from a lady that I'd never met in my life. I walked over to the couch and sat down under the noisy air conditioner with Jenny following me still asking me "what happened?"

She turned on the TV and was going through the channels telling me they had a composite drawing already airing out of the suspect. I noticed this chubby blond guy, darting in and out of the kitchen - and this little skinny girl with glasses sitting cross legged on the floor in the corner by the kitchen's entrance. I looked at Jenny and answered her consistent, non-stop questioning and hysterical babbling. "I didn't do anything! It wasn't me! I wasn't there! I didn't see anything and I don't know nothing about it." I didn't know what to do.

I was trying to watch the young man, trying to understand what had happened. Was this going to be the end of me? I thought about footing it to the bus station. No, this was serious. I didn't do anything, so they would have to figure out who did. I just kept my mind focused on that... let the police do their job and, in the end, they'll figure out I wasn't part of any crime, so just do what you know and keep your mouth shut. Let whoever is responsible take their own weight for their actions. I didn't do anything!

The chubby blond-haired guy turned out to go by the name Andy. Jenny and him kept walking back and forth from her bedroom door off the living room to the kitchen entrance, staring at me and the young man. Babbling non-stop, Jenny moved back inside her bedroom door so the young man couldn't see her and caught my attention by waving her hands at me. Once she had my attention, she started to spell something out in the air with her finger but I had no idea what she was trying to say.

I finally lost my composure because she wouldn't give me a second to think so I yelled at her, "Jenny! Sit your stupid ass down somewhere and shut the fuck up!" I couldn't handle any more of her in that moment. She stomped out of the doorway to the kitchen as Andy followed her. That's when I made eye contact with the skinny girl with glasses who was still sitting cross-legged in the corner. She said, "Hi, my name's Dawn" so I replied "it's nice to meet you Dawn, I'm Ira." She said she knew and wished we were meeting under better circumstances because "things are fucked up!"

I pulled my weed out and started to roll a joint. I was freaking out inside and couldn't calm myself down. The young man had been sitting in that chair the whole time, hands gripping the arm rests. I couldn't see his face though because his hair was covering it entirely. As I started to light my first joint, he got up and walked through the French doors of Jenny's bedroom and into the conjoined bathroom.

I couldn't help it; I got up and followed him into the bathroom. Not even knocking, I just walked in. He was at the sink with his hands on the sink rim with the water running. Before I could close the door, Andy had followed behind me and was trying to push his way into the bathroom. I grabbed him by the face and pushed him back into the bedroom where Jenny was standing as well. I closed the door and turned to the young man but he just kept looking down at the sink.

All I said was for him to own his own shit and leave me the fuck out of it. Then I opened the door and walked out, having to push past Andy and Jenny whom were in the process of crowding the door to eavesdrop but weren't prepared for me to be done so quickly.

Chapter 6

I just sat under that noisy air conditioner, smoking weed and waiting for the police to kick in the door. Jenny and Andy had come out to the living room after investigating whatever was going on in the bathroom. Jenny said she had seen him washing blood off his hands and Andy said he had seen the same. They were both claiming they had seen blood all over his clothes. Jenny told me that that was what she was trying to spell in the air with her fingers earlier - that he had blood on his clothes. I didn't see anything, having been lost in my own head praying that no trouble was going to spill over onto me.

Jenny then tells me that her and Andy were going out to find some cocaine or meth but I could see that Andy was all of a sudden trying to hurry up and get out of the house. Sure enough, within two minutes they were out the door.

Jenny returned twenty or thirty minutes later without Andy. She said they couldn't track the dealer down. I was just smoking weed, sitting under that noisy air conditioner. Once in awhile, I'd look over to check on Dawn who was still holding down that corner. Jenny came over to me with some pills, saying she could see how stressed out I looked and that these would knock the edge off. I asked her what they were and she replied that they were Thorazine and Xanax. She explained how she took them all of the time and that they took the edge off... so I took the four pills without any more thought.

She had sure down played their effect. I continued to smoke but I began having trouble keeping my eyes open or maintaining a thought for too long. I wasn't feeling well at all. Things were getting blurry. I was thirsty and my stomach felt unsteady so I got up and stumbled to the bathroom.

The door was locked and I heard Karen saying that she had just gotten out of the shower and would be right out. Up until this point, I hadn't heard or seen Karen since she was somewhere else in the house. I wasn't sure if I was going to use the toilet or if this was going to come up. With one hand on the door frame and the other clutching my gut, I stood there trying to steady myself. No, it was going to come up, for sure.

When Karen finally opened the door I blew past her, closing the door and went for the toilet. Before I even made it to my knees, vomit came up. The first burst mostly making its way down the front of my shirt and top of my pants. I stayed there in front of the toilet until my stomach was empty and the dry heaving stopped. I had made a mess of myself.

I got up and rinsed my mouth at the sink and tried to clean the vomit off my clothes but it wasn't working. I cleaned up my mess around the toilet as best I could before taking off my shoes and socks to get in the shower. The vomit cleaned from my clothes pretty easily but now my clothes were soaked. I stripped myself naked and left everything in the shower. Drying off with a towel, I went to my room and got dressed again in clean, dry clothes.

I remember wanting to smoke more weed and thinking about sitting under that noisy air conditioner so I walked back to the living room and sat in my spot.

Everything after that went blank.

Chapter 7

It was a crazy dream, my body was convulsing out of control and I could hear my name being called, "Ira, Ira, Ira." Then my chest hurt. I was moving but I was asleep. I kept trying to open my eyes but my motor skills were bogged down, then again, but really clear, "Ira, Ira, Ira", someone was on my chest trying to wake me up. I finally was able to open my eyes and there was a blur of a man, then focus came and this man had his knee on my chest, his other foot on the ground and was jumping up and down on me to wake me up. He had a 9mm in his hand pointed right at my face, he told me that it wouldn't be a good idea to try anything. As I took in the rest of the scene around the man on my chest, I could see five other guys standing behind him in a semi circle, all with 12 gauge shot guns pointed at me. Then I realized I was in the bed in my bedroom but I didn't know how I got there?

The detective that woke me up by jumping up and down on my chest told me we were going to get up and walk to the living room. I tried but just couldn't function so he and another plain clothes officer positioned themselves on either side of me and walked me into the living room and to my spot on the couch under the noisy air conditioner where they sat me down. Next thing I know, he's shaking me awake again and they help me up to cuff me, then assist me out to the back seat of an unmarked car. I was out again. My next memory was of the same detective waking me up and trying to get me up so a man could look at my face. The car door was open and I seen we were parked in front of the store, the detective was telling the man to take a good look but all he could say was "it might be the guy", then the detective saying, "Oh it's him, but we'll see you back at the station."

Next time I come too, they're trying to get me out of the car and into the station. Once inside they took me straight to a small room and told me they needed all of my clothes, then they took clippings of all my fingernails and pulled hair samples from all sides of my head. Standing there naked as can be, one of them brought in a camera so they could take pictures of every part of my body.

Some jail clothes were brought in and while I was getting dressed with three plain clothes officers in the room, they started asking me questions about what happened and if I was ready to give my statement. As I got dressed, I told them I didn't know what they were talking about, that I didn't do anything, I didn't see anything, and I don't know anything. They had me sit in a chair next to this small table while the three of them peppered me with questions and threats. The one that woke me up was saying they already knew everything so I better help myself out and get ahead of this by giving them my statement. I told them the same answer, I didn't do anything, I didn't see anything and I don't know anything. That's when my rights were read to me and I was advised that I was being arrested for robbery and murder.

They tried to drill me some more but I just kept making them mad by stating the same thing over and over. I didn't do anything, I didn't see anything, I don't know anything. Then they were threatening me with the death penalty, that if I keep on this track and not own up to what I did and tell what I know that they would make sure the D.A. pushes for the death penalty and, me being from out of state, I would be sure to get. I kept the same response but was also asking when I could be taken to the cell? I was told when I started to cooperate, and they were off with the same barrage of questioning. My answer was still the same but I was still feeling like, "blah", sapped from those pills and they were irritating me so I started being a smart mouth. I thought they'd send me to a cell but they continued pressing so I took it up a notch by asking what his wife looked like and if she still looks good naked. I pushed even further with sexually explicit innuendos and the lead detective got so mad he told them to get me the hell out of there.

I was placed into the federal holding tank with guys awaiting court dates for their charges. I slept all until the next afternoon, only getting up for my first court hearing where I met my court appointed attorney. When I did wake, the other guys introduced themselves, told me my name had been on the radio since my arrest then showed me the newspaper with my picture taking up half the page. The young man's small photo was set inside the article. The picture the article painted was that me, (a Mexican gang member from California), came into town and corrupted this small-town youth by involving him in the murder of the clerk.

Chapter 8

Every time I spoke with my attorney, he would push for me to accept a plea deal. I told him to look at me as I spoke the words that I need him to hear: "I did not have anything to do with any part of a crime!" So, he asked me to tell him what had actually happened then, since I was innocent, and said that whatever I say to him was confidential because every attorney is bound by "attorney-client privilege."

I then told my lawyer everything that I've already written in this book up until this point, even more. I told him all that I could recollect, leaving nothing out.

Hearing my version of events, he said we need to issue out a statement because the young man had already given four <u>different</u> statements, but in all of them he blamed me for everything.

I said to my lawyer then what I say here to all of you now... I will never tell on anyone, for any reason. I know this may not sound like something you want to hear, or you may not agree with me, but it is against my personal beliefs as a man. I have paid heavily to maintain these beliefs; I have paid with my life. But it is God's responsibility to hold people accountable and punish them for their actions. God's, not mine.

Once you've compromised your beliefs for a personal advantage, every other compromise becomes easier to make... until there's nothing left of you anymore but a rat.

I understand how horrendous this crime was; I also understand how God sees all things and will judge all people. Nobody will escape the eye of God. I'm sorry, but I've never been willing to compromise with these beliefs, ever.

My lawyer ran the same arguments at me I'd heard before, suggesting I that do myself a favor and save my own life to gain back my freedom. "Not going to happen, Bob." I've been honest about all of my actions and intentions, even when I didn't have to be, but understand that this is why I skipped over parts of the events of that night intentionally. I've stuck to my personal beliefs to this very day.

Within this book I've disclosed facts discovered by other people because it's what someone else already stated and can easily be found in the public record. A lot of people through the years have given me that same "you're crazy" look.... that look that says they'd have ratted on their own mother to save themselves or gain some advantage... but during these moments is when I see the price forever carved into somebody's forehead - the price at which they would sell out another human for their own personal selfish gain.

There is no law in any of the statute books that says "remaining silent is a criminal act." In fact, the American Constitution was set forth by our founding fathers to protect us from being forced to inform on our neighbors. We're supposed to be promised this right, without any retribution from the government if we so choose to practice it. The police are very capable of solving crimes...all they must do is the job they're paid to do. But to this very day I am serving a life sentence simply for practicing my 5th Amendment right to remain silent.

Anyways…

The news, radio, and newspapers were having a field day with my name. The local paper even published an article warning the citizens of North Platte to be on guard for any suspicious "out of state" license plates because they'd received reliable information that "Ira Leon's gang was on their way to North Platte to bust him out of jail."

I learned from a prosecutor's witness that the newspaper was being fed these delusional conspiracy theories directly from the District Attorney, whose wife conveniently worked for the newspaper as a photographer. Talk about having the ability to spin fake news!

After a trip to court, my lawyer made a visit to the jail to inform me of a local reporter whose name was being added to the witness list because she claimed that after she asked me a question, I turned to her and said "if you do what I did, you'll make the news." Her statement implied an admission of guilt.

Bob was furious! "What are you doing saying things like this, Ira?!" Initially, he believed that I'd actually made those statements to this reporter because, like everyone else, Bob didn't believe that a reputable news reporter would lie about

something like this. But the sad truth is...
they will. And they do - all the time.

Here's the catch... the county jail is
across the street from the courthouse so
every time I left for court or to see the
judges, I was shackled at my hands and
ankles before being escorted by two armed
deputy sheriffs. I was never alone; there were
always these two sheriffs who would hear
any statements I made to anybody. A sheriff
would be on each side of me, arm in arm, as
we'd come out of the jail and walk down the
steps to the corner cross walk. After waiting
for the crossing sign to signal "walk", we'd
cross over four lanes of traffic, then walk up
the street half a block to the courthouse.
Reporters may have been around but I was
never alone to speak to them.

I told Bob that I had said no such
thing! I explained to him that I don't speak
to anyone about anything and all he'd have
to do to verify my truth was to question the
two deputies who had escorted me that day.

The very next day, Bob came to see
me again and said "the funniest thing"
happened after he questioned those two
deputies (who verified that at no time did I
speak to anyone, let alone what this reporter
claimed I said to her). He received a call
from the district attorney who let him know

that the reporter had retracted her statement
against me.

Imagine that.

Chapter 9

I was only in the County jail there for a little over two weeks then they transferred me to Lincoln's Diagnostic and Evaluation Center to be held there under safekeep number #2458. They moved me, stating I was too violent of an offender to be held in the County jail with the other people awaiting court dates.

Still in North Platte, Bob continued to push for me to accept a plea deal. The Judge, had me brought over to his chambers at the courthouse. He sat behind his desk, the D.A. sat in a chair to the right in front of the desk, Bob and I took two chairs to the left of the desk with my two escorting deputies standing behind me a few paces. The Judge stated it was his understanding that I refused to cooperate, not even to save myself from the charges. He told me I should really reconsider my position to defend myself against what the young man was accusing me of doing. He even told me they know it didn't happen the way he was saying because all the evidence they've collected for his review goes strictly against his claims.

Then I asked what do they need me to tell for? He said that there was still the issue of the robbery and that the D.A. had filed felony murder charges on me. He told me to hold on a moment, that he wanted to bring someone else into this conversation, and I heard my mom's voice over the speaker phone. They had my mom on the line listening the whole time. My mom sounded very stressed as she begged me to tell them what they needed to know. I stuck to what I believe and told my mom "I don't know anything, you heard them yourself mom, they have all the evidence they need to get the one responsible. They're pushing on me to tell them what they already claim to know and I don't understand that." Our conversation continued in that manner but once they saw the back and forth wasn't going to change anything, the Judge thanked my mom for trying, then disconnected the call. He asked Bob if I understood the felony murder charge against me and Bob responded that he'd been trying to get this across to me but I wouldn't budge.

The day after the meeting with the Judge, I was taken to an interview room where Bob was waiting for me. He had a big red 1983 Revised State Statutes book with a piece of paper marking a place in it. He said to me that he understands that I'm trying to fight being any part of the murder but that's not what the D.A. needs to prove. I asked him if that meant they dropped the murder charge against me and he said "no, Ira, I need you to read this state statute before we talk more."

He opened the book to where the paper was marked and turned the book for me to read. *State Statute-303, Murder in the first degree (B) a murder that took place during the commission of an underlying felony such as a rape, robbery, assault, burglary, kidnapping, ect.* Then he asked me to read it out loud to him so I did. I said O.K. but I still didn't do anything, I didn't rob or kill anyone, I wasn't part of a plan or conspiracy to commit any crime and no matter what you or anyone else says, I want to go to trial to prove that I am innocent of any crime. By this time Bob had already shared the evidence collected in the case and it all proved I wasn't there and I didn't have anything to do with the crime.

All of my clothing had come back negative for any blood evidence, but the young man had blood all over his clothes. They impounded his car and took it apart piece by piece, they found blood all over the driver's side, door handle inside and out, one the steering wheel, down on the brake and gas peddles, even a plastic bag from the store with a bloody smeared print on it under the driver's seat. The Passenger side had absolutely nothing on it. There were no fingerprints of mine on the register or anywhere else and there was no evidence of me or from me in the store and nothing from the store on me because I didn't do anything associated with committing a criminal act of any kind.

Bob asked me to read the statute again so I did. But this time he looked at me and said, "Ira, the D.A. has evidence that the money was taken out of the cash drawer, he has this other guy that has given four statements claiming you robbed the store and killed the clerk ready to get on the stand and say this to a jury, and you refusing to give testimony of any kind to dispute him." He continued… "Ira, all the D.A. has to prove, all he's going to prove is that a robbery occurred, that this other guy will take the stand to state you robbed the store. The actual murder does not matter, even if you never got out of the car, you'd still be guilty of murder under the felony murder law because the D.A. just has to convince the jury that a robbery occurred."

I had taken my stand and I was going to stick to it because right is right, and wrong is wrong. I didn't commit any crime. Not only that but they had all of the evidence proving who did what and who didn't. The Judge had even sent the young man to Heartland Counseling and Consulting Clinic, to evaluate him because of his behavior in the jail, where he stated that the only family member that had ever showed real love to him was his "grandfather who had been murdered by an individual who had beaten him with a tire iron." "With all the information they had, they still want to charge me because I won't tell? No, we're going to trial Bob."

Chapter 10

They had to transfer me back and forth to court hearings from Lincoln now and that was over a four-hour trip one way. One of my court dates in April of 1992 got heated because the Judge asked Bob why he was asking for another continuance. Bob told the Judge he was having trouble getting depositions after your Honor denied his motion for an investigator, plus he was also in the midst of a murder trial in Hershey, Neb. The Judge started to press back on Bob about depositions not taking that long, even if he had to track someone down, since he could subpoena them. Bob replied, "your Honor, the D.A. has 140 witnesses on the witness list and I have to depose them all since I have no idea what any particular witness has given statement to?"

The Judge asked the D.A. why he had 140 witnesses when there is only one witness against me, that being the young man. The D.A. spit out some b.s. lines about all of them being crucial in their own regards but the Judge wasn't having it. He ordered the D.A. to revise his witness list into three categories in line with the witness' importance to the case... A primary, a secondary, and custodial. He also ordered him to list all 140 witnesses and list a brief summary next to each witness' name in regards to what the witness has given statement to. He also ordered that this be completed and submitted to the Court, as well as to my Counsel, within 30 days from that day's date. The Judge spoke to Bob about his order and Bob said it was fine, however, he wanted it noted that the court would have him relying on the D.A.'s point of perspective when it came to the importance of what any of the witnesses were witness to. The Judge stated again that in his order to the D.A. he made provisions for the D.A. to add in a summary next to the name of all 140 witnesses exploring what their statements consist of.

The D.A. jumped in and stated he will gladly comply with the courts order, he also further stated in open count that he had basically opened his entire file up to counsel in full compliment with the rules of discovery. This was just another court hearing of jousting between Bob and the D.A. to me. I wouldn't realize the importance of this hearing, the judge's order, and the withholding of two very Crucial Statements that without question proved there was never a robbery, until I filed for DNA testing under the DNA Testing Act in 2009.

I went back and forth to these court hearings waiting for the trial to start but each time Bob would have a conference with me in the law Library room in the courthouse to lay out his reasoning why I needed to accept the plea agreement or I would end up on death now. We'd argue for long stretches before we were forced to attend the hearing and each time, Bob would request for a continuance. The Judge would inquire about the existence of a plea agreement and Bob would tell him that his client was made aware of the plea deal, but insists he wishes to go to trail because he is innocent of the crimes charged against him. Bob even stated he made me swear of the possibility of being sentenced to the death penalty. This was during the request for the last continuance. The Judge asked the D.A. if he was seeking the death penalty. The D.A. stated that if I chose to go to trial that, yes, the state would be seeking the death penalty.

Bob came out to Lincoln to see me the following week and we spoke at length about every single thing and option surrounding the case. Even though I had nothing to do with this crime, in any way, I couldn't overcome the D.A.'s case of a robbery being committed. Money was missing from the cash register; the store owner confirmed the money was missing and had a total of the missing money from the receipts from that night. The young man was going to take the stand and say in open court that I robbed the store and all Bob could do was enter my statements into the record that "I didn't do anything, I didn't see anything. I don't know anything." I couldn't take the stand to personally say this or I would be subject to whatever questions the D.A. asked and I won't tell on anything! We couldn't even really speak of the non-existence of blood evidence on my person or anything from me at the scene because the D.A. only needed to prove that this robbery occurred. After nearly a year, I felt I had no other option but to accept this plea agreement that stated I could be paroled in 25 years.

Chapter 11

I went to court to change my plea and to accept the plea agreement. The Honorable Judge accepted my plea, however, he said he first wanted to contact NDCS, Nebraska Department of Correctional Services, to ensure that I would be able to attain parole on or before I served 25 yrs given that by law, he had to sentence me to life with the possibility of parole. So sentencing was put off pending the response from NDCS and the completion of a pre-trial investigation.

One day while in the unit at D&E I was called up for an attorney visit but when I got to the attorney/client room, there was a Hispanic gentleman who introduced himself as Arturo, a probation officer in North Platte. We sat down across from each other and he began to tell me that he's here to get my statement about the crime as he was pulling out a recorder and turning it on. He asked me to state my name, I did not respond. He asked me to go ahead and detail the events of that night as I recalled them, I remained silent. We stared at each other for a long moment. He started to say things that he'd read about me from my juvenile file and I continued to look at him without speaking.

Arturo then turned off the recorder and put it back into his briefcase, pulling out a pencil with paper. The same line of questioning followed with my same mute response. He was getting angry, started stating quotes of what the young man had stated against me, still receiving no response from me. He then began to tell me this has to happen, it's his job to get my statement and it will help me at sentencing so we needed to get through this because we are going to sit there as long as it takes to get it done. I told him to write this down, "I didn't do anything, I didn't see anything. I don't know anything" and if he wants to waste his time in a staring contest with me, to be my guest because I didn't have anything else to do besides go back to the Unit and lockdown in a Cell. We did sit there for nearly an hour, him talking, trying to find an edge; me just staring at him with my stupid smile. He finally gathered up his things and left while telling me how big of a mistake I was making.

The following week Bob came up to see me, we talked about sentencing; how to act and be respectful, and to go over what consideration he would be asking the Judge to take into account. Then he started pulling out some paperwork and told me that we needed to go over the statement I had given to Arturo for the sentence investigation. I said "What statement, Bob? I didn't give a statement." Then I told him everything that happened when Arturo came up. He showed me a statement, a statement that said, "as given by Ira Léon"? I flipped out! Bob tried to calm me down but I wasn't going for it, I told him I that I wanted this addressed with the Judge, and documented in court that this Arturo guy admitted a false statement into the Court.

The next court hearing was sentencing and Bob, at my angry insistence, addressed the court on record that I had an issue with this pre-sentence investigation statement by Arturo because it was not true and I had in reality refused to speak with Arturo during his visit. Court was put off while Arturo was located and he was then called to answer questions on the stand by the Judge. Arturo stated that I refused to cooperate with his investigation so he compiled my statement from police reports and the young man's statement. How could this fly? But it did, the Judge said it is on record that I refused to cooperate with the pre-sentence investigation which forced Arturo to compile a statement from official police reports and statements so they were willing to accept the statement as given to the court, my objection being noted.

Then the Judge read the response from NDCS into the record and had the State's seal stamped paper they responded on entered as "filed" which made it part of the record as well. He wanted to speak in regard to the response and why it was important to him. The Judge said under State Statute he had to sentence me to Life in prison with the possibility of parole, however, he was not comfortable doing so if I would not be released at some point on parole. He read from NDCS response that I could be paroled in 25 years if I maintained a job, completed all recommended programming, did not commit any acts of violence during my commitment, and served the last five years of the 25 years without a misconduct report of any kind. He spoke directly to me, telling me that I deserved to have the opportunity to earn my freedom, that he prays I take these stipulations to heart and abide by the rules that govern the prison I will serve my time at. He said I should be out on parole by my 49th Birthday, the same age as the deceased in this case. I was sentenced and transferred back to D&E to receive my inmate institution number, (#43804).

Chapter 12

I was transferred to the NSP (Nebraska State Penitentiary) on March 3rd, 1993 with four other guys about to start their sentences as well. I had spent the past year at D&E fighting my case so I knew a large number of people there that passed through D&E to their destinations. I was a good loyal friend to them during their time at D&E so, when I showed up, every curtesy was extended to me. I was even put in for a reclassification to a job in the shops of CSI (Corn Husker State Industries) two weeks after my arrival.

The pay wasn't much to a civilian but inside it was about the best you could wish for. I was hired in the license plate factory, I started out at 36¢ an hour, then after a solid month of a probationary period you get a bump to 54¢ an hour. You were stuck at this pay rate until you earned a 76¢ or $1.08 an hour spot, the latter being the top pay any inmate could achieve working at CSI. You could also earn a $500.00 bonus every three months if the shop you worked in cleared the quarter in the black. Working in the plate factory meant a guaranteed full $500.00 bonus every quarter.

I found my way down to the Law Library very quickly and had an older convict introduce himself to me as Jeff. He had followed the news coverage on my case and offered to show me how to obtain my court documents as well as read them over to find a way to get me back in court because I shouldn't be there for this crime. Jeff got me back into court via post conviction relief and I was granted a court appointed attorney on another motion he had me file. The only bad thing was that this newly appointed attorney was a no show. When the deputies came to pick me up to transfer me to North Platte for my post conviction hearing, the deputy introduced himself to me and showed me a big brown bag. He told me my attorney, (Leonard.) sent some depositions for me to go over during my trip to North Platte.

He told me that I needed to ride in front with him in his state issued white Crown Victoria with blue cloth interior. He got me into the front seat of the car, buckled me in then got in behind the wheel. It was already dusk and pretty dark out as we got to the highway to start our four plus hour road trip and he then proceeded to tell me that he had to have me in the front seat so I could help him navigate. Everything I am about to say is true, true, true and could be easily verified if someone wished to do the digging.

He told me that they called him in from home where he was recuperating from eye surgery for his cataracts! Not kidding you here at all. He told me it was a struggle to make the drive during the day but with it being so dark out now, he really needed assistance, so he asked me to let him know if he starts to drift out of the lane. Drift he did and I kept voicing to him, "off too far on the left… too far off on the right… you're crossing into the other lane.". He then did something that I will always remember with extreme pride and gratitude. He pulled off to the side of the highway, uncuffed my left hand, then tells me to just grip the steering wheel under where his right hand rested and help him drive straight basically.

We talked the whole way. He told me that he wasn't crazy and knew of the risk but it really wasn't a risk in his eyes because him and a few other law enforcement officers there in North Platte all agreed that

I didn't commit the crime I was in prison for. We ended up stopping at a Wendy's fast-food restaurant before we got to the jail and he said he was going to feed me good for the help and the good company. He ordered at the drive through but told the female voice on the speaker that he was in transport so he'd park then walk over to pick up the order. After parking in the corner of the parking lot, he got out to grab the order. I couldn't believe it, he left me in the Crown Vic. with a shotgun up on a blue clothed board that ran along the inside of the roof right behind the driver and passenger seats. It even had the black shell holder on the butt of the gun holding shells. And my left hand was still uncuffed. This was a good man. He was no fool, he knew the situation clear, he knew the character of the youngster he was transporting. We ate until I couldn't eat anymore then he re-cuffed my hand so all was right when we'd pull into the jail.

I spent three days in jail before my scheduled hearing and all I got from my attorney was another message that he'd be there to see me after lunch. He never showed up to see me. I was escorted to the courthouse three days later and this "oh so competent" attorney never spoke to me about our game plan. Yeah, I was already aggravated by this and one of the two deputies escorting me was being overly aggressive the entire walk. We went up the small maintenance elevator and I was brought into the courtroom through the side door. There were four chairs starting inside the side door, one right after the other, and, after the deputy took off my hand cuffs, per court order, he had me sit in the first chair right next to the open side door.

Within seconds of me sitting in that chair, the prick of a news cameraman was right there leaned inside the door with his camera inches, and I mean inches, from my face. This cameraman had followed me in this manner from the moment I was brought out of the jail and to the closing elevator doors at the Courthouse. I tried to speak with the cameraman, asking him to please give me some kind of respectable space, but he wouldn't even respond, just kept on filming. There were several attempts from me to ask for some personal space. The deputy standing just a few feet away watched with a smirk as this played out. As my requests were met with no regard, I asked the deputy instead if he could back this gentleman up a little. I even told the deputy that the cameraman isn't allowed in the courtroom anyway. He told me that I'd be alright. I tried to ignore it but with the camera lens actual inches from my face, I couldn't continue doing nothing.

I asked the deputy if I could move down to one of the other chairs but he said, "no sit where I put you." I met his gaze and stood up, telling him I'm moving to the next chair and he stepped towards me with his hand reaching out. I stopped and, looking right at him, told him to please not put his hands on me, I'm moving to the next chair. He hesitated for a few seconds, then grabbed me. I snatched all six foot two, 280+ Lbs. of this deputy into the air and slammed him down! I can still see his eyes as they grew as large as plates realizing he was in trouble. Pretty much every free body in that courtroom came running to try and subdue me. I was throwing and putting down everyone that came into my reach but I couldn't gain full control and neither could they. Even when the weight of all the bodies now involved took it to a ground game, neither side could take control. Finally, the very deputy I started this may lay with was tussling, close enough to me that he said "Ira, we can't get you cuffed, and you ain't getting away so if you'll stop fighting, I give you my word after you're cuffed nothing will happen to you" I was tired and had carpet burns all over so I told him lets do it. He called for everyone to back off me, and when it was just me and him he asked me to lay flat on my stomach so he could cuff me. This court hearing was in 1994 and the footage made the news for several days.

I was shipped back to D&E in Lincoln afterwards, not even permitted to attend my hearing which was denied. I made up my mind then that I would save every penny I could so I could hire a paid attorney. My first was John and it cost me five thousand dollars to retain him.

Chapter 13

Over a decade had passed since I'd been in prison at this point.

I had been writing to every Innocence Project I could find an address to, in any State, asking for help. John was on top of it. He couldn't believe what they had gotten away with doing to me. He had his investigators checking under every rock and his paralegals pouring over the transcripts. He came to see me for updates or to seek information as he and his team started to prepare to file my case in court. He was at it for nine months or better when he came to see me with bad news.

An attorney that worked for his firm had done some side work for the, Public Advocacy Commission, taking some depositions for a murder case that involved the young man they called my co-defendant. John said that he even presented the facts of it only being depositions to the president of the bar association but he was told his firm was in a conflict of interest and had to drop all dealings with my case.

He refunded me seventeen hundred dollars of the five thousand and we had to part ways. Yes, my co-defendant had been involved in the stabbing death of Kevin Goodenow at L.C.C. in 1994. He did the same case as he did in ours; he gave a statement blaming it all on his co-defendant/cellmate Jerry Simpson. Even though the evidence as I read it stated the victim was stabbed with two separate knives, the state accepted the young man's statement and gave him a plea deal that consisted of 20-life for second degree murder, and a transfer to Canyon City, Colorado to serve his time. Mr. Simpson was sentenced to death row and that's where the Public Advocacy Commission came in. They defended Mr. Simpson's case to be taken off death row and receive a life sentence instead because he had the mental capacity of a ten-year-old.

I put another five thousand together and hired this attorney out of Columbus, Nebraska that came at the recommendation of a "used to be" friend of mine, Paul. I met Paul at the prison. He used to be a case worker in the Unit I was housed in. Cheapest dude I ever met in my life but, at the time, a good solid friend. He was fired from the prison for stealing state clothing, razors, food, etc. If it saved him a buck, he'd take it. Of course, this attorney didn't pan out, he held up my money for a year and did zero work on my case, claiming he'd get to it once he cleared some of his existing cases. Paul even went to his office a couple of times and refused to leave until he spoke to him, but nothing came out of it.

In the end, I just had the attorney send my money back, which he did. Paul didn't do anything wrong to me but I cut all ties with him when a staff member came into my cell and laid an article from the Columbus paper down on my table and left with these parting words: "what do you think of your best friend now?" Now, I've met and kept in contact with quite a few staff members after they've left NDCS service and staff still in service pretty much hated me for it. The article left on my table was detailing how Paul was arrested in the parking lot of (I believe a beef plant, but I could be mistaken, I do remember it being the plant his wife worked at) a plant there in town selling methamphetamine to plant workers. He had assisted law enforcement in conducting a controlled buy on his dealer. I called Paul, read the article to him and told him "You know where I stand on snitches you rat bastard." I hung up and have never made contact with him again.

The entire time I never stopped going down to the Law Library to work on my own case with the help of some pretty savvy convicts well versed with the law and how to format, as well as file, in court. Working with one of these gentlemen, we took notice of the DNA Testing Act, which had been put in place by the Nebraska Legislature. We had everything submitted to the District Court but I was denied appointment of counsel, was denied the right to attend the hearing, and my motion was denied.

I filed for notice of appeal and part of that process is for the District Court Clerk to send me a complete copy of my Transcripts, and Bill of Exceptions and upon receipt of these is when I found the two statements that the D.A. and the North Platte police department had hidden from me and Counsil. The two statements that proved not only was there no robbery, but there was evidence in a criminal investigation not being collected, asked for, followed up on, and signed off on as being actually stolen from the store. I had been in touch with an, Innocence Project, out of Iowa, and the lady that ran it came to see me a few days after I filed my notice of appeal.

Seventeen years into prison now, I believed I'd finally received the evidence that would prove me innocent of "felony murder" and give me back my freedom.

Chapter 14

Okay... remember back in Chapter 10 when my lawyer had requested a "continuance of trial" because there were 140 witnesses to depose? - when the Judge told the D.A. to summarize each witness' statement on paper, provide me a copy of the summary, as well as divide the witness list into 3 sections (primary, secondary, custodial)?

Remember when the district attorney agreed to do so? - how my lawyer objected to this because we'd only be able to receive the state's version of what each witness said?

If not, please review chapter 10 again because it's the moment when the D.A. falsified police reports and intentionally withheld them from me for the next 17 years!

In 2009 is when I finally received this evidence for the first time.... but this information had been available since the first week of my arrest!

With all this in perspective, you're able to read for yourself the two statements in question. I've inserted them at the end of this chapter.

** Please take note that these statements are not stamped as "Filed by the Clerk of The District Court." That's because they were never turned over with the rest of the discovery evidence, which constitutes a Brady violation. A robbery charge filed against me even after they knew a robbery never occurred, used for the leverage of a "felony murder" conviction.*

After the two statements are inserts of the "primary, secondary and custodial witness lists", along with all 140 witnesses, accompanied by the summary of what each witness stated to police. These are the exhibits from when Judge R. ordered the D.A. to compose a summary so that we didn't have to continue trial and depose each witness separately. These exhibits were stamped as "Filed by the Clerk of The District Court" because they were provided to us. This is all we saw of each witness statement - the summary.

Take notice that ofc. Monte Vlasin is listed on the secondary witness list as "Number 15", but Mrs. Diane Sivits is not on any of the three witness lists! Now take note of ofc. Monte Vlasin's summarized statement, as given to the court by the D.A. (#53 on the list) and take note of Diane Sivit's summarized statement, as given to the court by the D.A. (#117 on the list).

Do any of these summarized statements accurately reflect the actual statements they made? - the actual statements which were hidden from the court, as well as from me and my counsel? Look at #53 and #117 of the witness summaries, then compare them with the actual statements included herein.

Why would the D.A. go through such illegal and deplorable lengths to ensure he had a false robbery charged against me? All ethical oaths out the window, just to hang me with the "felony murder" charge because, without it, they would've had to let me go free.

It took me quite awhile to actually perceive the magnitude of what this deception truly meant. All the way from who knew about it and helped keep it a secret, to who did not. Then, how do they pull something like this off? I mean, Mrs. Sivits went to the police station and gave her statement that evidence in an ongoing murder/robbery investigation was found by her, and the owner convinced the manager to hide the money in her purse and meet up with him later so that he could retrieve it from her! Not only was the money removed from a crime scene, they tampered with the evidence!

After Mis. Sivits gave her statement to the police, none of the investigators followed up to contact the owner or the manager to take their statements or to demand the money be turned over as evidence in an ongoing criminal investigation!

How does this happen?

Here's a real kicker...

A couple days after Mrs. Sivits gave her statement, the police detectives met up with the owner and the manager at the store so they could verify receipts of how much money was stolen from the register during the "robbery" and it was the exact amount Mrs. Sivits found! - but the police didn't ask about any of that. Not a word. They signed off on money missing from a robbery for the owner to file an insurance claim on as well.

Wow.

Bad tidings would befall the North Platte police department and the Lincoln County's D.A. office if any of this ever came to light.

I wrote to Bob about it, sent him copies and asked him if he knew about this? If he helped them do this to me?

My life meant so little, against what I still don't understand, because they had their man along with all of the evidence they needed to convict him... so why risk something coming out just to put me in prison too?

Voluntary Statement of Diane Sivits.

On 2-20-92 in the afternoon after 4:00 p.m. I was asked by Dee Harold Barn Store manager to come in and close. After being there for awhile everyone left, leaving Dee and I alone.

I went to bundle $20 Bills in $100 wrappers. When pulling out candy box containing the empty wrappers I found $524 in cash $1-$20 and check initialed by Betty C. folded on top inside box. I asked Dee "what's this?" She called John Haines (stone owner), explained to him we found some money it must be from Wednesday's drawer. She told him if turned over to police they would keep it till end of trial. This is all I heard of conversation, I don't know what happened to money. Friday I opened not having enough money. We start with $750 and I had only $504 so telling Dee she called John and then took a stack of bills from her purse told him she put it there and gave the difference to make $750 for today. Later John came to store and quietly said to me don't say anything about money the police found enough on the guy to nail him.

I'm lost why it wasn't found in search of premise. Box was turned around which ever was before, and bill and check folded and put in such a small area. Had to be put not thrown.

2-21-1992

VOLUNTARY STATEMENT

92-8902

d my address is Rt 1 Box 285 Hershey, Neb 69143

I have been advised and duly warned by ____________

who has identified himself as ____________
of my right to the advice of counsel before making any statement, and that I do not have to ____ ement at all, nor incriminate myself in any manner.

I hereby expressly waive my right to the advice of counsel, and voluntarily make the following statement to the aforesaid person, knowing that any statement I make may be used against me in the trial or trials for the offense or offenses concerning which the following statement is herein made.

I declare that the following statement is made of my own free will without promise or hope of reward, without fear or threat of physical harm, without coercion, favor or offer of favor, without leniency or offer of leniency, by any person or persons whomsoever.

On 2-20-92 in the afternoon after 4.00pm I was
sked By Dee Harold Barn Store manager to come in
nd close. After being there for a while everyone
eft. Leaving Dee and I alone
I went to bundle $20 Bills in $100 wrappers
henpulling out Candy box containing the empty wrappers
found $324⁰⁰ in Cash $1-$20 and check initialed By
etty C. folded on top inside box. I asked Dee "what's
his?" She called John Haines (store owner) explained
o him we found some money it must be from
Wednesdays drawer. She told him if turned over to
Police they would keep it till end of trial. This is
all I heard of ~~conversation~~ conversation. I don't
know what ~~happened~~ happened to money. Friday I
opened not having enough money. We start
with $750⁰⁰ & I had only 50¢ so telling Dee
he Called John and then took a stack of Bills
rom her purse told him she put it there and
gave me the difference to make $750⁰⁰ for today

ve read this statement consisting of __2__ page(s), and I affirm to the truth and accuracy of the facts
tained therein.

This statement was completed at 1815 M. on the 21 day of February 19 92

WITNESS: [signature]

DATE _______ TIME _______ PLACE _______

_______ Dale P. Swartz _______ am 38 years of age

d my address is Rt. 1 Box 285 Hershey

I have been advised and duly warned by _______

who has identified himself as _______
of my right to the advice of counsel before making any statement, and that I do not have to make any statement at all, nor incriminate myself in any manner.

I hereby expressly waive my right to the advice of counsel, and voluntarily make the following statement to the aforesaid person, knowing that any statement I make may be used against me in the trial or trials for the offense or offenses concerning which the following statement is herein made.

I declare that the following statement is made of my own free will without promise or hope of reward, without fear or threat of physical harm, without coercion, favor or offer of favor, without leniency or offer of leniency, by any person or persons whomsoever.

Later John come to store and quietly said to me don't say anything about money the police had enough on the guy to nail him.

I'm lost why it was found in search of premise. Box was turned around which ever was before. and bill and check folded + put in such a small area. had to be put not known.

I have read this statement consisting of __2__ page(s), and I affirm to the truth and accuracy of the facts contained therein.

This statement was completed at 1815 M. on the 21 day of February 19 82

WITNESS: M. Kern

WITNESS: _______

A Diane Sivits came to the station and said that she had something to tell me and that she needed to get this information off of her chest. She said that she did not know if this has anything to do with the murder that took place at the Barn Store but she needed to tell someone.

She said that on 02-20-92, in the afternoon after 1600 hours, she was asked by Dee Herold, the Barn Store manager, to come in and close. After Diane was there for a while, everyone left leaving Dee and her alone. Diane said that she went to bundle the $20 bills in the $100 wrappers and that when pulling out the candy box containing the empty money wrappers, she found $524 in cash in denominations of 51s, 5, 10s and 20s and also some checks. These checks were all initialled by Bettie Christensen, the victim of the homicide. The bills and cash were folded neatly on the top inside of the box. She asked Dee "what is this?" Dee called John Haines and explained to him that they had found some money and that it must be from Wednesday's drawer. Dee told John that if he turned the money over to the police, they would keep it until the end of the trial. Diane said that this is all she heard of the conversation and that she did not know what happened to the money. Diane said she opened the Barn Store on Friday. After opening, she realized she did not have enough money to start the day. Diane said that they usually start with $750 and this is in bills and in change. Usually they have $645 in bills and the rest of the remaining money is in coins. On that day, Diane only had $504 so she told Dee. Dee called John and Dee took a stack of bills from her purse and told John that she had put this money there and then Dee gave Diane the difference to make up the $750. This would be $145 in cash to make up the difference, leaving the remainder balance of bills in Dee's possession.

Later that day, John came to the store and quickly said to Diane, don't say anything about the money. Police found enough on the guy to nail him. Diane said that she is lost in why the money wasn't found in the search of the premises. The box that Diane said is used for the money wrappings where this money was found was also turned around backwards. She said that this box has never been like this before. Diane said that the bills and checks were folded and put in such a small area that they had to be put in, not thrown in. Diane described this box as being a candy box which has four sides. The top has been cut off and on one of the ends, a notch has been cut and bent as to allow a finger to grasp the box and pull it out from the shelf. The notch is usually turned to the outside as to be able to grab the box.

Diane said that the box sits in such as a spot as not to be in the view of the public eyes and that she has to bend down to get the box herself. She said that the box is located on a separate three- stack shelf which is located on the bottom shelf of the main counter on which the register sits. The candy box sits on the top shelf of the three- shelf stack and is pushed back far enough so as the public cannot see this box. Diane said that she does not know if Bettie was the one that put the money and checks in this box or not and that if it wasn't this, then she cannot figure out why John is keeping the money quiet. Diane said even though she works there, she does not care if they fire her over this as she had to tell someone about this to clear her conscience.

IV

IN THE DISTRICT COURT IN AND FOR LINCOLN COUNTY, NEBRASKA

THE STATE OF NEBRASKA, Plaintiff,	)	Case No. 105-276
v.	)	PRIMARY WITNESS LIST
IRA LEON, Defendant.	)	

FILED
1992 MAY 28 PM 4:04
ANITA R. CHILDERSTON
CLERK DISTRICT COURT

1. Stacy Fletcher
2. Byron Barksdale
3. Ron Blevins
4. Douglas Tethey
5. Gary Hovey
6. Shelly Jungck
7. Kim Jungck
8. Keith Davis
9. Bob Zeiler
10. Jim Roblyer
11. Rick Ryan
12. Jim Carmen
13. Gail Reed
14. Don Staroska
15. Jeff Foote
16. Steve Toelle
17. Rich Thompson
18. Rod Christensen
19. Chris Jarvis
20. Andrew Segan
21. Pat Pfifer
22. John Haines
23. Clint Jensen
24. Am-Britte Hillistad
25. Jenny Hyce
26. Ann Shrewsbury
27. Nebraska State Patrol Crime Lab Personnel
28. Rick Most
29. Jobe Castor
30. Christopher Foust
31. Gerald Rounsborg
32. Warren Orr

DATED this 28th day of May, 1992.

KENT D. TURNBULL #17435
LINCOLN COUNTY ATTORNEY
LINCOLN COUNTY COURTHOUSE
(308) 534-4350

EXHIBIT
7

106

IN THE DISTRICT COURT IN AND FOR LINCOLN COUNTY, NEBRASKA

THE STATE OF NEBRASKA,   )   Case No. 105-276
)
                Plaintiff,   )
)
        v.   )   SECONDARY WITNESS LIST
)
IRA LEON,   )
)
                Defendant.   )

1.   Joan Perry
2.   Ron Haggard
3.   Great Plains Regional Medical Center Personnel
4.   Irma Valentine
5.   Rodger Green
6.   Bruce Marksen
7.   Steve Hambek
8.   April Campbell
9.   Tom Sweet
10. James Ady
11. Dick Hough
12. Dan Barker
13. Lemoyne Daily
14. Matt Phillips
15. Monte Vlasin
16. Jon McNeel
17. Ron Jensen
18. Larry Gosnell
19. Dee Harold
20. Dick Odbert
21. Jeff Hedgecock
22. Lincoln County Jail Personnel
23. Clark Masters
24. Troy Tickle
25. Rich Hoaglund
26. Kendall Allison
27. Steve Armester
28. Randy Billingsley
29. Terry Falkena

         DATED this _____ day of May, 1992.

                                   ____
                                   KENT D. TURNBULL #17435
                                   LINCOLN COUNTY ATTORNEY
                                   LINCOLN COUNTY COURTHOUSE
                                   (308) 534-4350

107

IN THE DISTRICT COURT IN AND FOR LINCOLN COUNTY, NEBRASKA

THE STATE OF NEBRASKA,)   Case No. 105-276
          Plaintiff,)
)
        v.   )   CUSTODIAL WITNESS LIST
)
IRA LEON,   )
)
          Defendant.)

1. Western Pathology Services
2. Nancy Splichal
3. Larry Becvar
4. Jo Ashburn
5. Pony Express Personnel
6. Russell Leth
7. Larry Palmer
8. Bluff-Co Personnel
9. John Briseno
10. Leroy Swain
11. Deb Knight
12. Andre Adkin
13. Gene Jenkins

      DATED this _____ day of May, 1992.

                          KENT D. TURNBULL #17435
                          LINCOLN COUNTY ATTORNEY
                          LINCOLN COUNTY COURTHOUSE
                          (308) 534-4350

IN THE DISTRICT COURT IN AND FOR LINCOLN COUNTY

THE STATE OF NEBRASKA,	)	Case No. 105-276
Plaintiff,	)	
v.	)	WITNESS LIST
IRA LEON,	)	
Defendant.	)	

1. **STACY FLETCHER:** Mr. Fletcher can testify to items contained in the reports currently in the public defender's possession which detail Mr. Leon's involvement in the killing of Bettie Christiensen.

2. **BETTIE CHRISTIENSEN:** She is the deceased and will obviously not testify but evidence will be introduced concerning her death as contained in the reports.

3. **GERALD ROUNDSBURG:** A doctor at the Great Plains Regional Medical Center who can testify as to the results of the X-rays performed on Bettie Christiensen.

4. **WARREN ORR:** A Doctor at the Great Plains Regional Medical Center who can testify to the results of the X-rays on Bettie Christiensen.

5. **GREAT PLAINS MEDICAL CENTER PERSONNEL:** Individuals not yet listed on the Information that may be called, such as nurses, doctors, emergency room physicians, anyone who was present and had custody of certain items of evidentary value.

6. **BYRON BARKSDALE:** The pathologist who conducted the autopsy of Bettie Christiensen. The doctor can testify to items contained in the autopsy report.

7. **ERMA VALENTINE:** X-Ray technician who took the X-rays of Bettie Christiensen. Can testify as to procedure and methods and the taking of the X-rays.

8. **ROGER GREEN:** X-Ray technician can testify as to procedures used and the taking of x-rays of Bettie Christiensen.

9. **LYNN HANLAN:** Director of medical records at the Great Plains Regional Medical Center. Can testify as the custodian of records of any and all records that may be introduced as evidence.

10. BRUCE MARXSAN: Lab technician at the Great Plains Regional Medical Center. Can testify as to analysis of materials submitted such as blood.

11. STEVE HEMBECK: Lab technician tested Bettie Christiansen's visceral fluid which can determine the time of death.

12. APRIL CAMPBELL: Lab technician tested Bettie Christiansen's visceral fluid to determine time of death.

13. RON BLEVINS: Fresnic pathologist from Scottsbluff who examined the brain of Bettie Christiensen and can testify to items contained within his report.

14. WESTERN PATHOLOGY SERVICES: Employees of Dr. Blevins who may have handled evidence submitted by Dr. Barksdale to Dr. Blevins for examination.

15. NANCY SPLICHEL: Mailed Bettie Christiensen's brain to the fresnic pathologist in Scottsbluff.

16. LARRY BECVAR: Also involved in the mailing of the brain to the fresnic pathologist in Scottsbluff.

17. JO ASHBURN: Lab manager at the Great Plains Regional Center.

18. PONY EXPRESS PERSONNEL: Employees who transported the brain of Bettie Christiensen from Great Plains Medical Center to another facility for transportation to Scottsbluff Pathology Services.

19. RUSSELL LETH: Employee of Pony Express, can testify to transportation of Bettie Christiensen brain.

20. LARRY PALMER: Employee of Pony Express, can testify to transportation of Bettie Christiensen brain.

21. BLUFFCO COMPANY PERSONNEL: individuals who transported the brain of Bettie Christiensen from Ogallala to Scottsbluff.

22. JOHN BRISENO: Pony Express personnel employee, can testify as to the transportation of Bettie Christiensen's brain to Scottsbluff.

23. DOUGLAS TETLEY: Witness at the scene of the crime, can testify as to going into the Barn Store and observing Bettie Christiensen lying on the floor in a pool of blood. His statements are contained in Gary Hovey's police report.

24. SHELLY JUNGCK: Can testify to going to the Barn Store and observing no clerk on duty and also checking to determine if Ms. Christiensen was still alive. Her statement is contained in Gary Hovey's police report.

25. KIM JUNGCK: Was present with Shelly Jungck, can testify to observations made at the Barn Store and the victim Bettie Christiensen. His statement is contained in Gary Hovey's report.

26. ROGER WYATT: Can testify to arriving in the Barn Store with several other subjects while they were on brake from the Union Pacific Railroad. These individuals were there for a short period of time and were present during the time Bettie Christiensen was at the Barn Store and prior to any crime taking place. His statements are contained in the report by Gary Hovey.

27. LARRY HOLMQUIST: Can testify to being with Roger Wyatt and others at the Barn Store prior to the crime being committed. His statements are contained in Gary Hovey's report.

28. ROBERT COLEMAN: Mr. Coleman was also with Mr. Wyatt and Mr. Holmquist prior to the crime being committed. His statements are contained in Gary Hovey's statement in Gary Hovey's reports.

29. JEFFERY ROBERTS: Was also present with Roger Wyatt, Larry Holmquist, Robert Coleman prior to a crime being committed. His comments can be found in Officer Hovey's written report.

30. ANN LLOYD: Can testify to observations made in the area of 306 South Bailey in the alley next to the residence of 309 South Dewey. Can testify as to a grey car believed to be Stacy Fletcher's vehicle racing up and down behind the Hyce residence at approximately 10:00 to 10:30 p.m. in the evening. Further information is contained in Gary Hovey's report.

31. IRIS LLOYD: The sister-in-law of Ann Lloyd and can testify to the same things as Ann Lloyd as contained in Officer Hovey's report.

32. KIM ALEXANDER: The owner of the residence of 309 South Dewey occupied by the Ray and Jenny Hyce in which Ira Leon and Stacy Fletcher were present on the date in question.

33. KEITH DAVIS: A key witness in that he has positively identified Ira Leon as the individual within the Barn Store when Mr. Davis entered the Barn Store on the date in question. His statements are contained in the police reports. Initial contact was made by Gary Hovey.

34. A.J. GARDNER: A special agent with the Union Pacific
Railroad who made contact with Officer Gail Reed and advised that
four subjects Larry Holmquist, Robert Coleman, Jeffrey Roberts
and Roger Wyatt had been in the store previous to the crime being
committed. Mr. Gardner's comments can be found in Officer Reed's
report.

35. MARY ROBERTS: She is the wife of Jeffrey Roberts who was
interviewed by Officer Hovey, she was present at the time of the
interview, it is unknown whether she was present at the time when
the other four subjects were in the Barn Store. Her name is
found in officer Hovey's report.

36. RAY HYCE: The husband of Jenny Hyce who can testify that
Ira Leon is his brother and that he had been residing with them
for several days prior to the date in question. Information on
Mr. Hyce is found in various police reports beginning with
Officer Hovey's.

37. TOM SWEET: Lincoln County Sheriff's Deputy was present
during the search of the residence of Ray and Jenny Hyce and the
serving of the search warrant. His name is found in Officer
Hovey's report.

38. JAMES ADY: Officer of the North Platte Police Department
helped secure the crime scene at the Barn Store. His name can be
found in Officer Reed's report.

39. DICK HOUGH: Lincoln County Sheriff's deputy brought the
camcorder to the crime scene. On arrival Deputy Hough found that
the video was not operable and departed the crime scene.

40. DAN BARKER: Lincoln County Sheriff's Deputy who was present
with Dick Hough when a video camcorder was brought to the crime
scene and also was present when a search warrant was served at
309 South Dewey at the Hyce residence.

41. BOB ZEILER: An officer of the Nebraska State Patrol video
taped the crime scene as well as the autopsy of Bettie
Christiensen.

42. NORBERT LEIBEG: An Lieutenant of the Nebraska State Patrol
who came and made initial observations of the crime scene,
offered to lend assistance and initially conversed with Officer
Bob Zeiler on video taping the crime scene.

43. LAMOYNE DAILEY: A Deputy of the Lincoln County Sheriff's
Office who was present when a search warrant was served at the
residence of 309 South Dewey.

44. **JIM ROBLYER:** A police officer with the North Platte Police
Department who was present at the crime scene and helped secure
the area. He obtained evidence at the crime scene and the
autopsy of Bettie Christiensen. Officer Roblyer has a written
report.

45. **RICK RYAN:** An officer with the North Platte Police
Department can testify to statements made by Mr. Davis, as well
as to a verbal confession by Stacy Fletcher. Officer Ryan has a
written report.

46. **JIM CARMEN:** A lieutenant with the North Platte Police
Department can testify to an interview with Keith Davis who
observed Ira Leon within the Barn Store after the crime was
committed and further contact with Andy Segan who advised that
Ira Leon and Stacy Fletcher were at the Hyce residence at 309
South Dewey. Information obtained from Andrew Segan was used the
obtaining of the search warrant which Officer Carmen was also
present in serving the warrant at the Hyce residence. Officer
Carmen has a written report.

47. **GALE REED:** An officer with the North Platte Police
Department and was present at the crime scene and investigation
at the Barn Store on the date in question. Officer Reed also
talked to subject such as Darrel Damme and Don Damme, D.M
O'Conner and R.L. Dammet and Roger Herman. Officer Reed has a
written report.

48. **DON STAROSKA:** An officer at the North Platte Police
Department, who can testify to the crime scene investigation at
the Barn Store. The officer can testify to follow-up
investigation as to physical evidence submitted to the crime lab.
Officer Staroska interviewed Karen Hilstad about money sent from
the jail by Stacy Fletcher and various other follow up items
which are contained in written reports submitted by Staroska.

49. **JEFF FOOTE:** An officer with the North Platte Police
Department, can testify to transporting Ira Leon from 309 South
Dewey to an interview room at the North Platte Police Department.
Officer Foote gave Miranda warning to Ira Leon and made
observation of Ira Leon at that time. Officer Foote can further
testify to assisting in a search conducted by Officer Staroska in
area of Barn Store for evidence of the crime in which an "L"
shape tire iron was found by Officer Foote. Officer Foote did
give a written report.

50. **MATT PHILLIPS:** Officer with the North Platte Police
Department, can testify to transporting Stacy Fletcher to the
emergency room for obtaining samples of fingerprints, hair, and
blood. Officer Phillips can further testify as to items removed
from Fletcher upon incarceration in the Lincoln County Jail.
Officer Phillips gave a written report.

51. STEVE TOELLE: an officer of the North Platte Police Department, can testify to investigation of the crime scene at the Barn Store. The officer obtained evidence from Ira Leon at the Lincoln County Sheriff's office and collected other items at 309 South Dewey. Officer Toelle did give a written report.

52. RICH THOMPSON: an officer with the North Platte Police Department assisted with the search of the residence of 309 South Dewey. Officer Thompson further assisted in the gathering of evidence from the scene and Mr. Leon. Officer Thompson also talked to Rick Tilford and also presented a photographic lineup to Keith Davis and conducted an interview with Ann Shrewsbury of the North Platte Telegraph. Officer THompson interviewed several individuals incarcerated in the Lincoln County Jail that talked to Ira Leon. Officer Thompson did give a written report.

53. MONTE VLASIN: An officer of the North Platte Police Department received a statement from Diane Sivits, who is an employee at the Barn Store and advised Officer Vlasin as to how money is used to start the day at the Barn Store and various matters regarding money on hand. The statement made by Diane Sivits are contained in Officer Vlasin's report and written statements.

54. ROD CHRISTIENSEN: The spouse of the deceased can testify to the identification of Mrs. Christiensen as the person beaten to death in the Barn Store. Mr. Christiensen can further testify as to being in the Barn Store early in the evening having coffee with his wife.

55. CHRIS JARVIS: An E.M.T. employeed by the city of North Platte. He was on the ambulance crew that was summoned to the Barn Store on the night in question. His name appears in Officer Reed's report.

56. ANDREW SEGAN: An individual who contacted Jim Carmen of the North Platte Police Department and advised that he observed Ira Leon and Stacy Fletcher at the Hyce residence and that he received information that they had blood upon their persons and some money being taken. His interview is in Officer Carmen's report.

57. DARREL DAMME: A witness who spoke to Officer Gale Reed and advised that they had been at the Barn Store earlier that evening.

58. DON DAMME: A witness who was with his brother Darrel who made statements that they had been at the Barn Store previous to the time the crime was committed. His statements appears in Officer Reed's report.

59. D. M. O'CONNOR: A witness who works for the Union Pacific
Railroad apparently was driving an engine passed the Barn Store
at the time of the incident. His statement was given to Officer
Reed.

60. L. R. DAMMET: Mr. Dammet was a conductor on the engine with
Mr. O'Connor and could testify to observing a blue pickup with
white strips in the parking lot of the Barn Store as they went by
approximately 10:00 to 10:15 p.m. His statement is contained in
Officer Reed's report.

61. ROGER HARMEN: Advised Officer Reed that he observed an
individual in the alley around 2821 West 4th the night before on
2/18/92. His statement is contained in Officer Reed's report.

62. RICK TILFORD: Talked to Officer John McNeel of the North
Platte Police Department and gave information of an individual he
observed in the vicinity of the Barn Store around the viaduct
area. His statement is contained in Officer McNeel's report.

63. PAT PFIFER: Mr. Pfifer in talking with Officer John McNeel
advised that at the time of the incident, 10:00 p.m., observed a
1973 to 1975 primered grey camaro parked in the alley way near
the Barn Store. Mr Pfifer further indicated he saw one male
subject getting into the grey primered camaro. His information
is contained in Officer McNeel's report.

64. JON MCNEEL: An officer of the North Platte Police
Department obtained statements from Rick Tilford, Roger Harmen,
Pat Pfifer, and the husband of Bettie Christiensen, Rod
Christiensen. Officer McNeel further talked with R.W. Coleman,
George Trejo, Virginia Thomspon, Joey Zeigler. Officer McNeel
gave a written report.

65. GEORGE TREJO: A witness who stated that he observed people
in the Barn Store that caused concern to the lady at the counter.
She asked George Trejo not leave the area. His statement is
contained in Officer McNeel's report.

66. JOEY ZEIGLER: He was with George Trejo. His statement is
contained within Officer McNeel's report.

67. JOHN HAINES: He is the owner of the Barn Store and can
testify to the employees that were employeed and were on duty the
night in question He can testify to different accounting
practices and monies missing from the store. His statements can
be found in various officers reports specifically beginning with
Jon McNeel's.

68. JAMIE HORN: A witness interviewed in the presence of her father as statement made by George Trejo and Joey Zeigler. Her interview appears in Officer McNeel's report.

69. MICHAEL HORN: The father of Jamie Horn and was present during the interview of his daughter by Officer McNeel.

70. CLINT JENSEN: An officer with the North Platte Police Department who was present at the Barn Store at the time evidence was being gathered and did accompany the deceased to the funeral home at all times during X-Rays and autopsies.
He further interviewed several witness such as Pam Babcock and Edith Wheeler. He has a written report.

71. RON JENSEN: An officer with the North Platte Police Department who photographed the residence at 309 South Dewey and collected evidence found at the residence. This officer also collected physical evidence from both suspects Stacy Fletcher and Ira Leon and further assists Officer Staroska with the investigation. The officer made a written statement.

72. DEBORAH VON KOENEL: Probation officer of Ira Leon from California. Relatively little information is known from her at this time; however, her phone number and name is found in Officer Toelle's report.

73. MARTHA PRUIT: The mother of the defendant, Ira Leon, her name and number are found in the report of Officer Toelle.

74. LARRY GOSNELL: An individual who owns Larry's Glass and assisted in the removal of the glass doors at the Barn Store where fingerprints were found. His information can either be found in Officer Toelle's or Staroska's reports.

75. JANE TIGHE: Employee of the Barn Store.

76. DEB HAINES: Part owner of the Barn Store.

77. DEE HAROLD: Employee of the Barn Store, her name appears throughout the reports.

78. WILLIAM ROSS: The tow truck operator who moved Stacy Fletcher's car to the impound lot.

79. MIKE CHRISMAN: A mechanic for the City of North Platte who worked on obtaining evidence from Stacy Fletcher's vehicle with Officer Staroska. His name can be found in Officer Staroska's report.

80. DAWN DEWOLF: Shop forman under who Mike Chrisman works.

81. AM-BRITTE HILSTAD: A witness who received information and possible monies from Stacy Fletcher and who was also present at the time that Ira Leon and Stacy Fletcher came back to Hyce residence on the date in question. Her statement can be found in Officer Staroska's report.

82. CHARLES CLARK: Lexington Chief of Police who assisted Officer Staroska in finding Miss Hilstad.

83. DEB OURDALA: A Lexington Police Officer who assisted Investigator Staroska in finding Miss Hilstad.

84. MONICA PIERSON: An individual identified in Officer Staroska's report who supplied a residence for Karen Hilstad to stay at in Lexington, Nebraska.

85. GILBERT PIERSON: The husband of Monica Pierson who also supplied a place for Karen Hilstad to reside.

86. JENNY HYCE: Witness who resides at 309 South Dewey who advised both Officer Carmen and others that she observed the Ira Leon and Stacy Fletcher return to the house and saw what she thought to be blood on their person, they were acting strange and that they had some money that they didn't have previously. Her statements are found in Officer Carmen's and others reports.

87. NITA YANCY: Appears in Officer Staroska's report and she is the secretary of the personnel department in IBP Lexington and was able to determine work records of Stacy Fletcher.

88. APRIL PEARCE: She was a visitor at the Lincoln County Jail of Stacy Fletcher.

89. JERRY CHRISTIENSEN: Son of Bettie Christiensen.

90. RON CHRISTIENSEN: Son of Bettie Christiensen.

91. BRENT CHRISTIENSEN: Son of Bettie Christiensen.

92. KEN CHRISTIENSEN: Son of Bettie Christiensen.

93. LAURIETTA SAWYER: Visitor of Stacy Fletcher at Lincoln County Jail.

94. PAM FLETCHER: Visitor of Stacy Fletcher to Lincoln County Jail.

95. BRAD KOHL: Visitor of Stacy Fletcher to Lincoln County Jail.

96. BRENDA LEE: Visitor of Stacy Fletcher to Lincoln County Jail.

97. LAURIETTA DALE: Visitor of Stacy Fletcher to Lincoln County Jail.

98. DAVID PEARCE: Visitor of Stacy Fletcher to Lincoln County Jail.

99. DICK ODBERT: Lincoln County Jail supervisor, can testify as custodian of jail records.

100. JEFF HEDGCOCK: Assistant to Dick Odbert, can testify to jail records.

101. LINCOLN COUNTY JAIL PERSONNEL: Any and all individual who had contact with Stacy Fletcher and Ira Leon during this time who may have had statements made to them by either subject.

102. PAM BABCOCK: Advised Officer Clint Jensen that she along with Edith Wheeler had been at the Barn Store prior to 10:00 and had bought gas at that station.

103. EDITH WHEELER: Also gave a statement to Investigator Clint Jensen advised similar statement as given by Pam Babcock.

104. CLARK MASTERS: An officer of the North Platte Police Department assisted in developing a composite drawing of the individual seen by Keith Davis.

105. TROY TICKLE: Funeral home director with Carpenter's Funeral Home who assisted in the removal of the body from the Barn Store to the hospital and to the funeral home. His name appears in Clint Jensen's report.

106. CONNIE MCNEEL: Dispatcher with the North Platte Police Department. She received information from individual citizens as well as communications between the officer.

107. RICH HOAGLUND: An officer with the North Platte Police Department who was present during the search of residence of 309 South Dewey, was also present when trash was removed by Leroy Swain of the City of North Platte as well as traps that were removed from the residence by Steve Armester, a plummer in North Platte Nebraska. He gave a written report.

108. KENDALL ALLISON: A police officer of North Platte Police Department, can testify to an interview with a Jenny Hyce who resided at 309 South Dewey where Ira Leon and Stacy Fletcher had been residing. Further testify as to information from Karen Hilstad in reference to Stacy Fletcher. Also has a written report.

109. LEROY SWAIN: He appears in Officer Rich Hoaglund report as the individual who removed the trash recepticals from the residence where evidence was taken.

110. STEVE ARMESTER: Appears in Officer Hoaglund's report was the plummer who removed the trap sink from the residence of 309 South Dewey.

111. ANN SHREWSBURY: A reporter with the North Platte Telegraph who heard Ira Leon make a statement. Ann Shrewsbury's name and statement appear in Officer Thompson's report.

112. MAXINE CARY: A dispatcher with the North Platte Police Department obtained reports from individual witnesses calling in.

113. MARY DELUNA: A dispatcher with the North Platte Police Department obtained statements from various witnesses calling in.

114. BILL CARY: Mr. Cary called and talked with Mary Deluna and advised he had been in the Barn Store around 8:00 p.m. His statement is contained in Mary Deluna's handwritten report.

115. MERLE SOMMER: Statement made to Mary Deluna in which he had bought baby asprin from the clerk at around 9:15.

116. RANDY BILLINGSLEY: An officer of the North Platte Police Department who made contact with an individual identified as Rick Tilford who observed an individual north of 6th street on Buffalo parallel with the viaduct hiding behind a pillar next to front street. Officer Billingsley gave a written report.

117. DIANE SIVITS: Employee of the Barn Store who gave a statement to Monte Vlasin detailing some things that concerned her about the accounting practices of the Barn Store and the cash on hand and the location of where cash in kept. That statement is contained in Monte Vlasin's written report.

118. NEBRASKA STATE PATROL CRIME LAB PERSONNEL: Individuals from the laboratories in Lincoln, Nebraska who will be called to testify on custodial as well as evidenciary matters pertaining to evidence submitted.

119. JEFF PATTERSON: An employee of the Nebraska State Patrol at the Nebraska State Patrol Crime Lab. Unknown as to what he would testify to at this time since I have not received information from Jeff Patterson.

120. LINDA BOKOSKY: An employee at the Nebraska State Patrol who works in the crime lab. She came to North Platte, to use a laser printer to obtain fingerprints from the crime scene and other areas.

121.   RENA ROY: An employee at the Nebraska State Patrol Crime Lab, testifies to issues surrounding blood samples.

122.   MARK BOTANY: An employee of the Nebraska State Patrol Crime Lab in Lincoln, Nebraska, unknown at this time what he will testify to.

123.   MARK SOMMERS: A member of the ambulance crew that arrived at the Barn Store on the night in question.

124.   JOHN JONESON: A member of the ambulance crew that responded to the Barn Store on the night in question.

125.   RICK MOST: A member of the ambulance crew that responded to the Barn Store on the night in question.

126.   TERRY FAULKNER: Emergency Medical Technician, Not on duty that evening; however, lived in the vicinity and ran over to the Barn Store and determined whether or not the victim was deceased.

127.   EDWARD HANSEN: Tow truck operator.

128.   JOBE CASTOR: An individual incarcerated in Lincoln County Jail in which statement were made to him by Ira Leon. His statements are contained in Officer Thompson's reports.

129.   CHRISTOPHER FOUST: An individual incarcerated in Lincoln County Jail to whom Ira Leon made various statements which are contained in Officer Thompson's written report.

130.   DEB KNIGHT: An employee from Blufco Company that transported the brain of Bettie Christiensen to Scottsbluff.

131.   ANDRE ADKIN: An employee of Blufco Company, also who helped transport the brain of Bettie Christiensen to Scottsbluff.

132.   GENE JERKINS: An individual who may have also transported the brain of Bettie Christiensen to Scottsbluff.

133.   DAVID BAY: An individual in the Lincoln County Jail serving time with Ira Leon and Stacy Fletcher.

134.   DANIEL SERRANO: Incarcerated in Lincoln County Jail serving time with Ira Leon.

135.   JOAN PERRY: Member of the Nebraska Job Service who can testify that Mr. Leon had been in the Job Service on 2/19/92 and filled out a job application in that office. His information is contained in Officer Thompson's report.

136. RICHY MCQUISTAN: His name appears in Officer Thompson's report but contact has not been made with him.

137. JERRY LITTLE: A jailer at the Lincoln County Sheriff's office who received information from Jobe Castor about Ira Leon bragging about killing Bettie Christiensen. Information is contained in Officer Thompson's report.

138. DIANNA SNOGREEN: Unknown at this time

139. KEN HAGGARD: Can testify to being at the Barn Store earlier in the day and observed two individuals sitting at the table near the coffee machine. They appeared to be 18-20 years of age and possibly fit the description of Stacy Fletcher and Ira Leon. This statement is contained in officer Toelle's written report.

140. ROBERT KOFUT: A sergical associate of Grand Island Nebraska who was contacted in reference to a hysterectomy done on Bettie Christiensen to determine what type blood type the victim was. Mr. Kofut indicated that he had not done any blood work up and thus did not have her blood type. His statement is contained in Steve Toelle's report.

DATED this _____ day of May, 1992.

____
KENT E. TURNBULL #17435
LINCOLN COUNTY ATTORNEY
LINCOLN COUNTY COURTHOUSE
(308) 534-4350

A:J.E1-13

Chapter 15

After filing my notice of appeal, my case was picked up to be heard by the Nebraska Supreme Court and I quickly sent them copies of the two statements in the form of a supplemental transcript because I had already filed my brief to the court and I wanted the court to see these two statements for sure.

Well, I got an attorney visit from the lady from Iowa's Innocence Project during this time frame before my case was to be heard by the Nebraska Supreme Court. She brought another attorney with her, Tracey, out of Omaha. We had a really good conversation, they wanted to help me, they read through my transcripts and couldn't believe it. Then I showed them the two statements I found and, this is a truth, they won't even dispute, they were in tears. I'm talking flowing tears over what was happening to me, and how I've somehow found the will to keep fighting all of this time. The lady that ran the Innocence Project out of Iowa said they were in the process of trying to get an Innocence Project up and running here in Nebraska and that's when Tracey devoted her services pro bono to help out. They swore Tracey would be with me to the end, that she'd now take over my case before the Neb. Supreme Court, that she'd represent me for the 10-minute oral arguments and no matter what we'd push this to Federal Court and beyond until justice was served.

My case was scheduled to be heard before the Nebraska Supreme Court on a Friday, I couldn't wait to get back to the unit after work to call Tracey but it was late and I didn't get an answer. I came in at lunch from work that Monday to call her and she told me that the lower courts ruling was affirmed. She was crying telling me how oral arguments went. I asked what they said about the two newly discovered statements but she said through sobs that she never got around to bringing that up. I couldn't believe it, what were you talking about then? She said she was touching on the importance of the DNA testing which was what my appeal was on but the State Attorney generals brief was asking for the lower courts ruling to be affirmed because DNA evidence wouldn't prove anything that the state already didn't know in 1992, that I was not the one who committed the murder. So, DNA testing would not overcome the robbery portion of the crime that made me guilty of felony murder. She told me that the one Justice who did the speaking during oral arguments kept asking her, "but how do you get around felony murder?" I told her, "You're an attorney, you know he was toeing the line to prompt you to bring up the discovery of the two statements!" Through her tears she just kept apologizing and assuring me that we would file for reconsideration then go to Federal Habeas, that I had her all the way to the end and we'd prevail.

That was on Monday. When I came in from work Wednesday. (yes, two days later), the staff called me to the Control Center to sign for legal mail. It was from Tracey and her law firm. The letter said she was so sorry but her firm will no longer allow her to pursue my case pro bono so she is removing herself as my counsel and wishes me all the best in my pursuit for freedom and justice. I did my best not to let my mind wander with conspiracy theories but all I could think about is who got her and what did they say to scare her off my case? I couldn't help but think that, because, how could she go from the compassionate, caring attorney so filled with emotion and eagerness to fight for me, to this. I mean, the tears were real. All this up until Monday and I get this two days later. That meant she had to have written it on Monday, or Tuesday at the latest, for me to be getting it on Wednesday. What could have made her do such a complete turn around like that? I was hurt for sure but every time I take a punch it just makes me fight that much harder!

Chapter 16

I thought long and hard about how I could get this newly discovered evidence in front of a court that would look at it from the actual view point of the law. This guy that was assisting me brought up the idea of filing a state Habeas as to bypass the lower court of Lincoln County that didn't want this coming to light under any circumstances. We took our shot but it was denied and affirmed, but it gave way to file a federal Habeas next.

When I received the response to my federal habeas filing, I was in segregation, the year was 2013. I was so happy I yelled, "heck yeah!" at the top of my lungs! The judge ordered a hearing because "all three of Mr. Leons claims are cognizant and warranted review". My happiness was short lived however because the prosecutor filed a summary affirmance. His claim was that I shouldn't be allowed the "three-day mailbox rule" (which would make my filing late and legally out of time). Yes, the "three-day mailbox rule" was put in place lawfully for incarcerated litigants that are filing on their own behalf pro-se, giving them three extra days past a due date to account for the mail system in prisons potentially taking longer than usual to be mailed out. So, for the second time I was now fighting a case in court, but not my case. I was fighting to prove the prosecutor was incorrectly stating my filings were late.

Everyone reading this is probably thinking, "no big deal", but you would be gravely wrong in that thought. The prosecutors know that this is anywhere from a 2–3-year ordeal for you in court with mass amounts of continued filings, and court hearings always set 8-10 months apart from one another. It's the "wear you down" tactic. I would always read about the three prongs for this or that to prove certain stances in a court of law and "due diligence", was always there. Due diligence actually means to continue allowing the court system to steal more and more years of your life before they'll finally permit justice to take up review of your issues so when they have to overturn your case they still got all, or most, of the time out you anyway.

As sure as the sun rises and sets every day, only those with enough money to pay for private attorneys that can call in favors from prosecutors, or judges from the same alma maters, or that came up in those same close circles of friends, can count on true swift justice in their favor. You have the right to believe otherwise, you have the right to believe the scales of justice weigh out the same for one and for all but all you have to do is open your eyes to see the truth. It used to be hard to unearth because it was always done so far back in the shadows, ever so quietly, but just review the last few decades, especially this last one. The crooked have boldly stepped out into the bright light and dare anyone to dispute "their truth." They lie, they steal, they corrupt everything and everyone they come into contact with. All they do is point the finger at others, talk in circles while they cater to people's fears, then offer relief from those made up fears and people come in masses to stand by them, to fight for them.

Back to the "time-bar" fight. They kept me in court into 2017 before I sat down with another convict that assisted me in legal matters when I would hit sticking points like this. He suggested that we just let this case go so I'm not just spinning my wheels fighting for my case to be allowed to continue beyond the late filing motions the prosecutor put in the mix to gum up the works. Years keep passing and I've yet been able to actually get these two statements, newly discovered, in front of a court to have them seen and adjudicated lawfully.

So instead, I decided to start over by filing under "newly discovered evidence" in the lower District Court back in Lincoln County. My motion was denied claiming my motion, under newly discovered evidence, was "not the proper vehicle" to bring my issues before the court. Of course, we followed through and filed for notice of appeal to have the Nebraska Supreme Court look at it and they affirmed the lower courts decision.

After doing some research to find the proper vehicle to get my case before the court, we decided to file a motion to "withdraw plea, or successive motion for postconviction relief" and we filed this on February 4th, 2019. Of course, the District Court denied the motion, not because this wasn't the proper vehicle, but, because the Honorable Judge (a new judge that took the place of the previous Judge) sided with the District Attorney's belief that the evidence I was putting forth didn't support my motion. So, I filed for notice of appeal inside the slotted 30 days, but the Nebraska State

Penitentiary was so displaced with how it was run day to day that I had to make a stand on the 28th day into the 30-day time limit just to have a notary made available to me.

I get my case manager to finally take notice that I had been attempting to get down to the Law Library to have my documents notarized so I could file them. Usually, the Law Library and the Unit managers were certified notaries however at that point in time the prison had lost most of their staff and the notaries that remained had not been in the facility for some time, for reasons I was not made privy too. Only the law librarian was able to notarize but he was making us wait until our unit's yard #2, (odd days), had library to access him. Only for the couple of weeks I tried to get my now completed notice of appeal notarized, he was not on site during our scheduled yard #2 time slot. So, I wrote an Inmate Interview Request, (I.I.R.), asking to be placed on pass to the law library but he had it set up so once your I.I.R. was received, he'd schedule you for a week and a half later. The facility became aware and continued to allow him to act in this manner. The Prison's Court Liaison, Lannette, was very helpful to me in every way and she was a notary but she had been out on leave for personal reasons.

On June 28th, 2019 I finally was able to have the case manager call up front to the Administration to explain the time sensitive situation and as if they could contact the law librarian to inform him so that he would call me down to notarize my court documents that day. I went down and got the notaries, then paid for copies and ran back to the unit to personally hand my case manager the two manila envelopes that contained my notice of appeal addressed to the Lincoln County District Attorney, and the other to, The Clerk of The District Court of Lincoln County, so they could be mailed out before the 30-day deadline which was the following day, June 29th, 2019.

I received the letter from the Nebraska Supreme Courts Clerk on July 27th 2019 stating they are in receipt of my Notice of Appeal on July 24th 2019. I've been filing court documents for years now and knew immediately that this was impossible, it should have been filed as in receipt of June 29th 2019. So, without question the Nebraska Supreme Court was going to dismiss my case for being filed out of time. This had to be a joke, staff personally took those manila envelopes to the mailroom to be sent out on June 28th 2019 so how did it take nearly a month to get to the Nebraska Supreme Court Clerk?

Chapter 17

Due diligence, they just keep on punching me and I keep getting right back up, but it is getting harder, and harder to do. My appeal was denied for being filed out of time so I had to do the research and write up more motions to file, to fight for the third time now, to have my case reinstated inside the slotted time frame. Again, I am fighting in court over "time frame" and not my actual case. By this time, I had had a few conversations with the facilities court Liaison, Lannette, and she set the stage for me to always have access to her for notaries or any legal questions I may have, as well as to keep on the same page about upcoming court hearings. She's the one that advised me to write the mailroom for confirmation on the date they mailed out my notice of appeal, which should have been on June 28th 2019.

She led me correctly as the facility has to keep a log of all incoming and outgoing legal mail for a set number of years for situations just like this. Of course, the District Court denied my motion claiming I didn't mail in my notice of appeal when I claimed I did. I filed notice of appeal on this ruling and within two weeks of my filing, the Nebraska Supreme Court sent my case back to the lower court with direction. They even ordered that I be granted an attorney to assist me in my case.

I was given an attorney, Patrick, who came to the prison immediately to see me. Yes, another attorney that is worth his salt! We talked and he was ready to get my case reinstated and get my actual case back in court to finally be heard. He told me the I.I.R. from the mailroom wasn't enough, that we needed copies of the actual log. I let him know that Lannette had already talked to me about this and advised me to have you subpoena them because the facility can not give me personally copies of the logs, but they can give them to my attorney. So, he noted this and told me to just be ready for my scheduled hearing in May of 2021 and he'd take care of the rest.

When my hearing date came, I was in Lannette's office sitting right next to her in front of the computer screen. The call connecting us to the scheduled hearing came through but for unknown reasons the visual with zoom was not hooked up for my hearing. The Judge spoke and stated how this would go and how he wanted everyone in their turn to state their full names for the record. Lannette spoke up and introduced herself but asked the Judge if she could speak in regards to the serving of the subpoena the previous week. He let her speak and she told him she is the court liaison here at the Nebraska State Penitentiary and that when the deputy sheriff came the week before to serve the mailing logs, he spoke with the Cpl. posted at the front entrance and he called her to notify her of his presence and need to see her. She said she told the Cpl. she'd be right there but when she got through the security stations to get to the front entrance, the deputy had just left the subpoena with the Cpl. and took off instead of officially serving her in person.

Her issue was acknowledged by the Judge and she notified the Judge that the mailing logs in question were already in route to the court via U.S. mail and that she put them in the mail personally. My attorney introduced himself as did I, then Lannette and lastly the D.A. My attorney laid out our case for reinstating my notice of appeal, then the Judge asked the D.A. if the state had anything to say. She said, "no your Honor." There was nothing to argue. I proved that I placed my notice of appeal into the U.S. mailing System on June 28th, 2019. The Judge still said at the end that he would officially rule on the case when he was physically in receipt of, "Exhibit 119", the mailing logs. Lannette spoke up again to state for the record that she had personally made copies of the mailing logs and placed them in the U.S. Mail to the court. He adjourned the hearing pending the Courts receipt of the mailing logs, stating he would make his ruling at that time.

Things took a turn for me while I was waiting for his ruling, outside of anything to do with my case. In June of 2021, actually June 18th, an incident occurred on the yard. It was a Friday and I was standing out in front of the turnkey in the front yard. A fight broke out between two guys and after the staff responded to break it up, they ended up with two staff trying to restrain one guy and five staff on the other guy. There was a staff member holding both his arms and both of his legs and the fifth staff member laid across his chest. Well, the guy with only two staff trying to restrain him broke loose in an attempt to continue his attack but he bumped the fifth staff member laying on the other guy's chest, as more staff already on route got a hold of the continued aggressor and pulled him back. The fifth staff member freaked out at the contact and tussling going on. He turned back and forth for no reason other than being in fear, started to punch the defenseless convict, being held down by four other staff, in the face. I took off at a run across the front yard screaming for the staff to "get the fuck off of the guy" to which made the freaked-out staff member pause as he watched me branding towards him. Other staff took advantage of the pause and pulled him away from the convict. I reached the scene and was on the dude for being a piece of pussy shit for what he did. The other staff encircled him and rushed him across the yard and into turnkey before he got attacked in retaliation for what he did.

Monday morning on June 21st 2021, a half hour before scheduled movement, nine staff members had my cell door opened, then advised me I needed to let them handcuff me so they could escort me to turnkey. Once in turnkey, I was locked into a holding cell where I sat from 5:45am to 1:20pm when two staff appeared in front of the cell door bars dropping a black bag full of transportation restraints. I was transferred to TSCI (Tecumseh State

Correctional Institution) along with an M.R. (misconduct report) for apparently inciting a riot. At this point I was approaching my 30th year of incarceration and know a lot of staff, and a lot of staff know me. So, when I went to my IDC (Institutional Disciplinary Court) hearing, I was standing in front of a lady that has known me for 27 of my 30 years in here. She dismissed the M.R. in its entirety but I was not welcomed back to NSP because of my alleged self-destructive actions, and behavior, over the last couple of years.

Chapter 18

Since the moment I entered the prison system, I have carried myself in a certain way. I have always held a job, always stayed out of things that were none of my business, however, if there was even a hint of trouble, I'd be there quick fast and in a hurry to end it. Color of race never meant a damn thing to me, and I sure didn't care what gang someone was in. If you were a good solid man with similar morals and values, I made it a point to introduce myself. We were the few, that was very easy for me to see, so I figured it would be in our best interest to stay in communication with one another, keeping a constant flow of knowledge about any and everything.

As the years past, I had come to be known as the guy you could always get a fair shake from, the one that really hated bullies and would intervene when I seen someone worth their salt (in my eyes) being prayed upon. I am known for being brutally honest, and would get to the bottom of hearsay by dragging all parties involved into a "face-to-face" conversation, which in itself quickly brought the bullshitter to light. If you were a worker and needed help getting a job, I'd get you hired working with me in the shop. Though I have to date been hired (24) times, and terminated (25) times from the shops, I always get back in because of my known work ethic and ability to manage whatever comes my way.

I ran the plate factory as lead-man from 1995-2011, and that consisted of the entire license plate factory, the welding shop, and the point stop. The shop Supervisor would wait for me to come in to make sure he unlocked everything I'd need open, then go read his newspaper and make phone calls throughout the day. In 2002, April 23rd to be exact, I was shipped to TSCI with all the other max custody convicts to fill up the newly opened facility. The plate shop had a pretty new Supervisor, Tim, and he told the NSP Administration that if they transferred me, the shop couldn't run and that he'd quit.

Well, they do what all Administrations do, whatever they want, and I was sent to TSCI with a going away present from the Major and his henchman Captain. They felt the need to stand in front of me while dressed in full transfer jewellery to let me know they were the ones who ensured my transfer and how glad they were to be getting rid of me. They wished me the best of luck trying to introduce all of my drug contraband into this new Supermax prison that was built for scum of the earth like me.

Not trying to take you off track, just want you to know and understand a little bit about the man writing this. Prison is prison, and you either figured that out right now or you got ate up and I mean, not just physically. I've seen dudes get broken, that "far away, never to return" look of a now mentally unstable shell of a man. Yes, there are many men out there right now that could stand up and attest to the fact that if I didn't intervene to help them during their time incarcerated that they wouldn't be who they are today.

On the other side of that, yes, I was rightfully hunted by the Major, and his henchman, a Captain, because I was the guy that introduced contraband of every kind within NSP. I didn't care what you wanted, if you could foot the bill, I'd get it in. I justified what I was doing by my simple understanding that I needed to make the kind of money that would help me pay for an attorney.

The Major. and Captain's happiness were short lived though. They didn't really grasp the fact that the license plate factory was an actual business and that businesses needed someone to run it or it didn't run. The plate shop went into a dead stand still, no orders were filled, no plates were being made and the geniuses that were hired in our place started taking the machinery apart claiming that was the issue. Tim stuck to his threat and quit two weeks later. After nearly three months of not being able to produce one single license plate, and nearly a million dollars in lost product from the workers running unusable laminate and steel through the cutting press, staff at the DMVs scattered across 93 counties got the Governor involved! The Governor in turn ripped the NDCS Director's ass and he had the deputy Warden from TSCI come down to CSI Laundry to ask all the convicts that worked at the plate factory to be transferred back to NSP to get the plate shop back up and running.

When he came to my work area where I was already lead-man for the personal clothing accounts, I told him, "No, thank you." He couldn't believe it, he said, "but you'll be sent back to NSP, everyone else has said yes, yes, yes and there's only five spots." I told him again, "no thank you." You see, I was doing just fine where I was at! Already lead-man at work, already had avenues bringing in black market items, plus, I lucked into a relationship with my case manager, Angela. Are you kidding me? I was in heaven! Yes, I say heaven and my religious devotion and beliefs are what caught Angela's attention from what she told me. I've always been a believer, God is at the forefront of my life, though there were ups and downs where my faith waivered. I didn't go to their scheduled church sessions, didn't do Bible Study, I didn't walk around with my Bible, didn't attempt to bring others to faith through conversation. I read my scriptures each and every day in the solitude of my cell, I get on my knees each and every morning to give thanks and praise to my Lord and my God, in the secrecy of my cell. My relationship is with God, no one else. She was able to sneak peeks at my activities as most staff do while doing area/safety checks.

Three days later I was called back to the unit from work, and when I got to the unit, the unit manager was calling me into his office where Angela sat crying. I was lost in a rush of brain activity over how to handle this, and what had she already admitted to? The unit manager, Mr. B, proceeds to tell me to have a seat but he's side eyeing Angela with a weird questioning look. Then he hands me a piece of paper telling me that I was one of the lucky ones that made the list of five for transfer back to NSP to work in the plate shop. Now I understood. I just stayed focused on Mr. B because he was clearly trying to figure out what the heck was going on with Angela. I told Mr. B that there was a mistake because I was the only one that told the Deputy Warden that, "no, I had no wish or desire to go back to NSP", so they needed to correct this mistake and send one of those other dudes bent on going back.

A couple of hours later I was called back to the unit but this time Mr. B tells me they know I said "no", but I was actually the only one they wanted. I tell him I'm flattered but let them know I don't want to go back and if they force me, I will not work in their shop. While he made some calls, I went back onto the unit so I could catch a few words with Angela. I tell her she can't get all emotional like that, for sure! Then we talked about what I'd do if they forced the transfer.

They weren't giving me a choice, Mr. B informed me that the top CSI

Administrator, Tom, insisted that bringing me back was a must or the shop wouldn't get running again. He said that the decision for my transfer was beyond just NDCS control since the DMV brought the issue to the Governor. Five of us were transferred the next day and, per the plan Angela and I came up with, I refused housing, forcing them to place me in segregation for transfer back to TSCI. They kept me in segregation with daily visits from Tom trying to convince me to help him get the shop running and train the new hires how to keep it going. Finally tired of my stubbornness, they let Tom come down to my cell one last time. This was my second week back, I told him sorry but no dice, I don't want to be here. The Major. and Captain were waiting at the door this time and once Tom walked out, they came in. At this point the Major spoke, "We don't want you here Mr. Leon, we thought we got rid of you." He went on to tell me how someone very high up made it possible for me to be back here against their wishes and if I want to be difficult and not come out of the hole to get that shop up and running, that I'd get my wish. That I'd be transferred back to TSCI in two, or three years and that I'd do them down here. Then they turned, closed the door and left. They had me with that one. The hole itself is nothing. It's the worst they can do to you and once I figured that out, it was easy to make any decision that could land me in there. The hole only adversely affects people who need other human contact, or attention of some kind, from anyone and in any form they can get.

But I went to the cell door and told the case worker to have them let me out. Not five minutes later the door was popped and I was given the unit and cell I was being assigned to. I spoke with Tom and the Major about twenty minutes later and, through hopefulness, requested to be transferred back to TSCI only once I had accomplished their goals and got their shop up and running and their new hires trained. To my surprise, they both agreed to this. However, I was not sent back to TSCI until June 21st 2021.

After I got the machines fixed, put back together, and the shop up and running with much needed plates headed out the door to the DMV's, I was asked to usher in new technology. A large area of the shop was cleared out and a temperature/climate-controlled room was built for the newly purchased three-quarter of a million dollar, DLP, machines to be brought in. As they were forklifted into place and all the big wigs gathered around, they all thanked me with these kind and heartfelt words... "We'll never have to rely on an inmate again." Go figure.

Chapter 19

When I spoke earlier about the staff in prison having concerns over my behavior those last few years, they weren't off the mark at all. I lost my Mom on October 16th 2017, and nothing, and I mean nothing, could've prepared me for the downward spinal I was about to take.

I walked around in a daze, not registering anything else going on around me. I would come and go on auto pilot basically because I had been doing the same routine for years. Whenever I was approached, it wasn't me they were getting. I was angry all of the time. At night I laid awake with tears streaking down my face. I stayed in heated conversations with God, I challenged Him, I cursed the day He brought me to this world only to put this on me. I had shouldered every single other burden placed on my shoulders but this one crushed me. "Lord, you assured me through scripture that you'd never place more on me than I could handle."

My friends (yes, I say friends because I don't believe they set out to do anything intentionally to harm me) tried to get me out of my own head by trying to get me high. I never did drugs… well… except pot, I smoked pot up until I was 25. Well, at 46 years old I got high with a couple of them and it was the worst thing I could've ever done! 2018, '19, '20, '21 was a haze of events for me, all I knew was when I got high, I didn't feel that pain anymore and that made me dangerous. You were going to give me what I needed to stay in that haze or it would get very bad for you.

I was able to function on the daily. I went to work, I worked out, but the main goal was to keep the drugs in my pocket to use throughout the day. All those that knew me made it to one of two classifications; the true friends test who really struggled to see Ira in this kind of state and the ones who were gitty inside that they got to watch the great and renowned Ira become a mere junkie. I was all that, and knew what was on each individual's mind. I was messed up and really hurting but it didn't make me a fool to what was going on around me. Over so many years of meeting and dealing with so many different people with so many different personalities, it was easy for me to read people and I'd do it as I stood there in front of them with the dumb smile I always keep on my face.

My Mom was my world, my Old Goat, the only person in this world that I could count on for any and everything. She's the one who introduced me to our Lord and God. She made sure that I understood the scripture from as far back in my life as I can remember. That was what made me so angry with God. I'd call her every Sunday and couldn't wait to hear her say "My Smira" in her broken English accent. I'd ask about my candle. She'd light a candle for me each week when she went to church and she'd tell me about the Holy Mother and the prayers she sent up for me, that soon I'd be home with her and she'd wait forever if she had to.

Yes, tears are streaking down my face this very moment. I've already had to splash cold water on my tear ridden face three times since I got onto this subject. I have no shame for the feelings of sadness or the tears they bring. I stand the man she brought me up to be. I feel, I love, I hurt and I am truly saddened for not having her in this world with me anymore. The emptiness it has left is what almost consumed me, but

God never turned from me, He waited for me to turn back to Him.

Though I was in such a zombie like state, I still bounced in and out of programs, which led me to people and those people to more programs so I could meet even more people. Even before I was kicked out of NSP, God was working to heal me. I just didn't know it or put the chains of events together until much much later. Of all people, the warden of NSP, Michelle, was the first to poke and prod me, seeing something was very wrong with me. She reached out to me and sent others at me to figure out what was wrong and how they could help me. Nothing came all at once is what I've now managed to put together. No, God just sent me in a direction, or others in my direction, to give me that little bump that wouldn't heal me but would touch me just enough to send me in a direction.

Through Michelle's actions, I met, and was brought in the program class for WRAP (wellness recovery action plan) with Ashley. The weirdo that wouldn't stop staring at me, she made me very uncomfortable and that's not an easy thing to do. She's not one of those women fresh out of university talking to people about what she read in a book, she's been through some of the worst that life can throw at a human being. She stands at a possible 4'11" but beams with the confidence of a giant and when we first talked, I could see clear the pain and trouble looming in her eyes. Then when she gave me her little smirky smile, I understood this slick little sucker was reading my own pain and troubles in my eyes. It turned out that Ashley is a person I count among my very few real friends. She engaged me. She challenges people just by her own strength to stand up and share her own personal trauma with one and all. Another bump that sent me in yet another direction.

These bumps came in many forms from different people, Lannette being one. I spoke of her earlier but she was there for me in more ways than just as the legal Liaison. She worked up front with Michelle and, as I should've known then, they had all been sharing their concerns for me. Lannette made it where I could have any staff call her at any time to speak with her and a pass would be issued, or if I was around the other kind of staff, I could just walk into the turnkey and have the Seargent posted there give her a call. We talked often and I'm very grateful to her for all the compassion she showed to me.

My boss, Justin, was another bump that sent me in another direction. He is strong believer in the Lord himself and he was another very receptive person God put me in touch with. We'd talk at length about all kinds of things, mostly about the actual job. He'd tell me, "Ira, you're the best and smartest worker I've ever come across, we have all our faith in your abilities and know it'd take five guys to replace you." We shared stories about our families with each other, shared the hurt and pain of our losses. The only thing that I wish I would've been strong enough to speak to him about at the time was my struggle with drug use. He knew about my Mom and seen what I was struggling with, but I was too ashamed to say to him that I was using drugs to escape the pain. Justin is another great person that I call a friend to this day.

Chapter 20

I was eventually sent to TSCI where I still struggled with my loss and the constant desire to dull that pain with drugs. They put me in a unit and on a gallery with two case workers that wouldn't give me a freaking break! They were on me from sun up to sun down! I couldn't fool them, they seen me in my true form because they'd both been there too. Two more bumps that sent me in another direction. They talked to me very bluntly, telling me they'd read my file, seen what I used to bring to the table, heard what kind of guy I used to be… so what happened? Why is this older man standing in front of us acting like he's not whacked out on drugs? Them two were more like a heavy nudge then a bump, but it sent me in yet another direction.

All of these bumps into other directions always led me to good people, people that showed me that they cared, that they wanted to see me overcome, to climb back up from where most had already written me off as forever lost. I started to see as I thought more and more about these encounters and relationships. It was picking me and I hadn't even realized it. I put in for every program they had to offer at TSCI. I got a job again and I made up my mind to stop using drugs, to take an honest look at those trying to help me, trying to educate me. <u>I had to give it all up or it wouldn't be a real effort</u> and I'd only be lying to myself. I was better than this, my Old Goat taught and expected better than this. I prayed every day but, in that moment, I asked God to help me stop sliding by, to please allow me to welcome my Lord and Savior into my heart, and my life. To strengthen me against the evil I allowed to dwell in my heart.

I signed up for ALPHA, a Christian based program that really brings it to the table. Eye to eye they meet with you, and speak with you as the equals we all are in Christ our Lord. The volunteers I met are just awesome and it was another bump I needed that sent me in another direction. I learned so much through these people, true workers of Christ. They made me see the good in myself again, the value I brought to the world and the work I could accomplish in Christ's name. All the while I had been growing closer to another convict we call Shadow. He was another person I was meant to meet, another bump that sent me in the right direction. Shadow is a whole hearted believer and it only takes one look at him to see God is working through this good man. He was everything that I needed and at the time I needed it. We shared scripture always, shared experiences and trouble spots. Without ever having to say it out loud, we knew we could count on each other and that God meant for us to meet when we did.

God loves to let us know that His hand has been guiding us, or those around us, the whole time. He did just that for me when I put in to become an Intentional Peer Supporter (IPS). They were running interviews at a set date and would interview whom ever put in for one of the 18 available spots. By this time, I had nearly eight months under my belt of keeping clear of drugs and I already knew that that dark part of my life was over. I was back to me and some. I had been picked out of the muck by my God and there was no going back. I took the bearing meant for me to take, I was humbled in every way, but here I was being guided out of the fire. I was ashamed of my fall at first but the further away from it I got, the prouder of it I became. I overcame. I was written off, yet here I stand stronger then ever. I learned from my fall. It has helped shape me into the man I am.

When I walked into the interview, guess who was one of the two ladies doing the interviews for IPS? Ashley! God is good! The little one with the strength of a giant, one of the first that assisted me down this path to be healed and become so much more. And it wasn't over. The other lady she introduced to me as Tessa. I had been sneaking peeks at her until I heard the name because she looked so familiar. Turns out, I did time with Tessa's dad in the 90s! Joe (Tessa's father), me, and a man named Richard were best friends and did everything together. I was on a good path and everything was coming together for me. My constant smile grew welcoming once more because it wasn't fake anymore! It was now coming from everything great in my life beaming from me in the brightest way.

I was chosen for one of the 18 spots to become IPS certified. I completed the 40-hour class and did my best as I stood, in front of one and all, to give my at least 5 minute speech describing what my understanding of the core IPS values were. Each day things just became greater and greater for me, and the best part of that journey for me was that I repaired my relationship with God. I begged for wisdom and understanding so that I may fulfill His will, and greatness just keeps coming my way. Before I take you on the very unexpected next turn that most would have seen as bad?! I didn't. I knew God was opening a door, or doors, that just weren't showing themselves yet for me. He will not let a single stone dash my foot and I believe that with all that I am. Here I was now, over a year past the moment I asked for the strength to step away from drugs, nothing but greatness coming my way. I had never felt so alive, so full of pride.

Chapter 21

Going back to my last case filing, the one that should've been an easy ruling for the Judge if he was only kind of "honorable" as his title claims him to be. In January of 2022, I received a letter form my attorney where in he's informing me that he can no longer be my attorney in this case because the Governor had appointed him a District Court Judgeship for Red Willow County. My mind automatically brought me back to thinking about these conspiracy theories instantly. Every time I got someone that read my case and wanted to help, something completely random and almost comical pulls them away from it.

I had been wondering what was taking the Judge so long to enter his judgement anyways. It was coming on a year since the hearing and he said he was just waiting on Exhibit #119; the mailroom logs which Lannette put into the mail a couple of days prior to the hearing. Then, on March 21st 2022, I receive legal mail from my new court appointed attorney, that he wrote dated March 16th 2022, providing me with a copy of the District Courts order from March 14th 2022, denying my motion. Get this now… The Honorable Judge denied my motion because he claimed to have never received the mailroom logs from NDCS and that NDCS stated they won't turn over the logs requested even under subpoena! Yeah right, logs that are kept under law for this one sole purpose.

This punch took the wind out of me! Not only is this Judge hiding his court's incompetence in handling the original notice of appeals timely filing, now he's denying the mailroom logs were ever sent by Lannette! Plus, this new attorney, Bronson, never got into contact with me to advise me he was now representing me until he sent the Judge's order. So, I write him a letter that day to get in the mail, March 21st 2022, telling him I want to appeal this crazy ruling and how he can personally call Lannette at NSP and she'll verify that she did in fact mail the Judge the mailroom logs. I also put in for Bronson's office phone number to be placed on my calling list so I could contact him. His number was approved and on my list for use two days later but when I called, no one answered. Not even a secretary. I called three different times that day with no response. I called the next day throughout the day and still no answer. I called the day after that with no answer so I wrote him again explaining the important of filing before my time was up and we were already 10 days into the 30-day limit. I called every weekday for four straight weeks and not once was there an answer. I wrote three letters to him in total with no response of any kind still to this day. These facilities have to keep logs of legal mail and legal calls. Everything I've said can be factually proven.

Waiting on this new court appointed attorney put me over my 30-day time frame to file my notice of appeal and I've been stumped since. How do they get away with their blatant disregard for the legal system that they all took oaths to uphold? I was considering writing a letter to the Nebraska Supreme Court explaining these events. Then I thought about it from their point of view. It's not their job. They only deal with matters of law filed in a proper lawful way. So, I haven't done anything since.

For some years now I've been trying to figure out how to get my case into the public eye. With all I read about the internet and technology, I know this is the way but I don't have the feet on the street anymore. An old staff member I have been in an on/off relationship with since 2003, Jessica, got back in touch with me and started coming up to TSCI to visit me every weekend for five and a half months about the same time as this last order came through from the Judge. I asked her if she'd seen what I sent her and put it out on the internet so I could get eyes on my situation. She said she would and could do anything and how easy it would be since she does her work from home on a beefed-up computer system that the company she works for has provided her. Like I said to start, on/off relationship. After that, she came up missing again. I'm not a presser. We're talking? Cool. You fall off the map? Cool.

I have a good brother that I met years ago. We got really close but he made his way through the system and back out to the streets. I heard about him often, but not from him, which is just life. No bad feelings. All who know me know just stay out there and live. That's enough for me, that makes me smile just knowing you're out there doing right and living life. Well, God's hand moved my brother, Weirdo Bill's, heart to reach out to me December 3rd 2023 and we e-mail back and forth ever since. Plus, now I call him up to check on him every Sunday night. He is another blessing. Are you seeing what I see now? All the little bumps from God have all added up to greatness for me and all who are around me. It is awesome.

My brother Bill has a lot heaped up on his own plate. That's why I've never asked him to help get my case on the internet. Friends know where each other are in the moment and don't take advantage of one another. But when you read this next chapter, you'll see it worked out and Bill's girlfriend, Morgan (really nice young lady, by the way), is going to help me put a completed file on the internet. Just wait and read what comes next. I told you things took a very unexpected turn that most would've seen as a bad thing…

Chapter 22

I was at TSCI doing everything right, spreading goodness around, helping anyone in need. I had a full IPS schedule of fifteen peers I was seeing each week for an hour session each time, at the least. I was working in the CSI laundry as a lead-man in the personal room and loved my job as well as the other inmates and staff that I worked with. My routine was set and I was in a very good place. I went to work Monday through Friday at 7:45am until 5:00pm, only leaving for my scheduled hour IPS passes. I had been seeing two peers each day, Monday through Saturday, and three peers on Sunday. I was happy to be making these connections and growing new friendships that we all benefitted from. For the ten peers that I would see on the weekdays, I had to clock out of work to see. That was costing me roughly 10 ½ hours a week, 42 hours a month of lost pay. I have no other means of income to support myself so willingness to give up $60.00 per month to attend my IPS scheduled sessions is all pro-bono clearly showing my belief in the IPS program itself.

My daily schedule was full and I had to sneak in the yards for my workouts whenever an opening came available. I work out in some fashion at least once a day, six days a week. I do no work of any kind on God's Day, the day of rest. Lockdown at TSCI is at 5:45pm and for the most part I'd be asleep by 6:30-6:45pm every night and up for the next day at 4:00-4:15am every morning. I get up to wash my face, brush my teeth, then I'd clean the sink, the toilet, wash the walls and the floor. Then I'd wash my hands seven times before I laid out my prayer rug, grabbed my Bible and rosary to pray as well as give all thanks and praise to my Lord, to my God. After this, I would get up to put all those things back away so I could make a cup of coffee from the sinks hot water. I spent 15-20mins doing stretching exercises then I would watch the news as I read 4-5 chapters of scripture. When my cellie would wake up, he'd get ready. Then we'd sit watching the news until the door opened at approximately 7:45am at which point I'd go grab a mop with a clean mophead and water to mop the cell out. Then I would go to the dayroom to do an ab routine on the table until they called work lines for CSI.

That was my every day and I felt very productive. I had really good relationships with a majority of the staff which made it a great environment. I hadn't had the opportunity to meet the new Warden or Deputy Warden yet though. They did their jobs in a different manner than the prior Administrators. The prior Warden and Deputy Warden believed in making themselves available to the inmate population as well as their staff. The Warden would be out on the yard every morning welcoming anyone to a conversation. He made sure that his Administration made themselves available as well. Once they traded Wardens out, it shifted right back to the same old. The administrators hid in their offices up front never being seen again. I couldn't point out the new Warden for parole.

Yes, I know you are waiting to hear about this unexpected turn of events that came out of nowhere! Well on August 14th, 2024, I reported to work at CSI laundry as usual. Every day I come in, I go straight to the personal room to push the packed clean carts for ENVH (Eastern Nebraska Vets

Home) out to the locked gate of the loading dock. Then I grab my cup for coffee. On the way out I grab four net bags and two "do not dry" bags, with two clean aprons to take back by the dock door where I will be sorting personal clothing for the two accounts we have: DCHC (Douglas County Health Centre) and ENVH. Then I go fill my cup with coffee as I greet everyone in route with good mornings, bad jokes, or conversations in regards to what pro team lost my money.

Within 30-45minutes, the first truck makes its drop at the dirty dock. There are six inmates that work the dock but only four inmates are allowed on the dock to unload the truck. Once empty and the roller outer door is shut, they let in the other two dock workers to begin the processing through the x-ray machine, then the sorting. There are a lot of guys getting paid to work at CSI laundry but only a handful of us that bust our asses to get the work done. We migrate with the work when we know we are needed. I used to sort the personal clothing on the dirty dock but when the six inmates rule started becoming an issue, I moved my process out to the side of the door that opens onto the dirty dock. So, pretty much every day I am filling in for one of the six dock workers that is out on pass for religion, programming, school, MCC classes, OSHA classes, etc. This has been my routine for nearly two years but on this day, August 14th 2024, when the lead dock worker asked me to come throw dirties onto the x-ray machine belt, things went bad.

The very first cart is always DCYC (Douglas County Youth Centre), I had thrown about 6-7 bags onto the belt when I hear CSI supervisor say that something looks like a tablet in one of the bags as the belt stopped. No big deal, this happens every day, we find phones, remote controls, spoons, forks, knives, keys on key fobs, electric shavers, wallets, rings, necklaces, etc. when the belt stops, I know we're looking for something and, per protocol, everything on the belt comes in reverse back to me and the last bag or two that was taken off the other side is brought to me. I then place each bag one at a time onto the belt with a 3-5 count space between each bag until the staff locates the bag with illegal items in it.

So, I started the process and after three bags I heard CSI supervisor say "there it is, it's in the second bag." Usually, they pull out the item and write down the name on the clothing item it came from or if found loose they write down where it came from then put it in a plastic glove until we're done. Then they'll fill out a form, place it into a manila envelope and send it back with the drivers. Not this though. When he was handed the item and raised it up in his hand, I seen a large item about the size of a footlong sub wrapped entirely in black tape. This was a problem. I've been around way too long not to know that! He got on his radio to call for immediate assistance on the dock and I heard the new young female corporal next to him say "I think I see phones", as she was looking at the packages. I held up my hands and asked Mr. Stenson what he needed me to do. He told me to wait for his call to be responded to, and as he was speaking three staff entered the dock area along with the CSI laundry manager, my boss Doug.

With the item secured and taken to a "staff only" area, my boss Doug stayed back with us to observe the rest of the process. They asked me to rerun every single bag one at a time from the DCYC account and once that was done, I popped up the cart so they could see the bottom. Then tilted it on its side so they could view the inside. The door was opened and the empty carts were pushed out with DCYC's laundry for processing into the washers. We completed running the entire DCHC account. Once it was sorted, the empty carts and clothing were pushed out to the washer side for processing. The five of us working the dock were shaken down and we left the dock area. I had to finish sorting the personal clothing now so I could get them started in the washers. Once finished, I always grab my extra set of clothes and wash up and change in the restroom.

An hour later while I was sitting in the personal room getting all the paper work completed for the day's accounts, the Sergeant approached me to inform me that my Unit Manager had called and needed to see me before count. As soon as I walked into the unit, she called me to where she sat behind her desk and turned a paper with pen towards me and said "I'm sorry Ira, but they're putting you on Administrative lay-in for something" I couldn't believe it! A lay-in meaning that I am unable to work. I didn't do anything other than my job so what the heck are they insinuating?

The next day I went out early to catch my boss, Douglas, on his way in. As soon as he saw me, he said "I know Ira, I know, wrong place wrong time" he tells me he knows I didn't do anything so just let them do their investigation. He said since I was the only one throwing the dirties onto the belt, that the Warden and Deputy Warden decided they wanted to be involved in this and thought it best to lay me in. He said they wanted a list of approved inmates that work on the dock and that they quizzed him as to why I was back there. He told them I work back there pretty much every day filling in where he needs me, but that wasn't enough for them. They wanted him to submit everything in writing.

I spoke with staff throughout the facility as the days went by and they all said the same thing. "Wrong place, wrong time" and to just let the investigation unfold and I should be just fine. The staff in the loop told me not to worry because they all watched the video and it was clear I didn't do anything but my job. Some told me the Administration was freaking out because they wanted someone to hang this on. I went on with every other part of my days, only that I couldn't report to work. So, I filled the time with working out, and reading my scriptures until one of my IPS passes came up. All I could do was wait for them to do the right thing.

Chapter 23

You're going to love their version of the right thing. On August 23rd 2024, ten days after placing me on administrative lay-in, I was on my way out of the unit to see a guy for a 2:00pm IPS session. Three staff closed in around me to tell me they needed to take me up to intake. I sat in a holding cell until a staff member came to the cell door to have me sign paperwork stating I was being placed on I.S. (Immediate Segregation) "pending the outcome of an investigation." Yes sir, ten days after this incident they now put me in the hole, still not even receiving an M.R. (misconduct report).

They had me go before their long-term restrictive housing committee, on September 6th 2024, two weeks after being placed in the hole on I.S. They asked me if I had anything to say to the committee. I responded "yes, I would like to know first of all why I am here and why am I here without an MR?" They said I was there pending the outcome of an investigation over the contraband found at CSI laundry on August 14th 2024. So, I stated to them what took place that day as I wrote it there for them to read. So why am I in the middle of this? They said they're only doing what they're being told. I asked "by whom?" but they would not give me any response. I asked them "If I'm here waiting for the outcome of an investigation for the incident at CSI laundry in which I still have not received a MR for, then why have my three immediate segregation reviews had under the "reason for placement" as "threats or actions of violence"? they told me that was put on my paperwork to justify holding me in IS by those that had me placed down there. I was like what? So, you're turning a blind eye to your superiors breaking the rules and violating my due process rights? "We're just doing our jobs, Ira".

The next Friday, September 13th 2024, I was transferred to RTC 384 special management unit in F1. While I was in intake with three other guys being dressed for transfer, I was chatting with a couple of staff I know very well and the one, my old boss from TSCI canteen, says to be good and he's glad to see I haven't lost my smile. The other asked "how can you be smiling still?" when I answered "Because I know I didn't do anything. I know people at central office are making these decisions, not caring if they are punishing the right people or not, they just want the population to see what will happen if you engage in this kind of activity. And what keeps my smile is knowing all these things combined, they're merely God's hand at work. What anyone else thinks, or believes, never has mattered to me. God and I know that I was doing great so He wouldn't let harm befall me. He was opening new doors for me. I just need to wait and see what they will open."

I get here and sure enough, I know most of the guys here, some I even seen for IPS sessions. God is good. He is all knowing. I was moved into a cell with a 26-year-old that was pending "bed space" at a halfway house as he had been granted parole. He wants to succeed. He doesn't want to be a statistic and he sought information from me that would help him overcome those fears. We talked at great length, shared much, I even got him a job opportunity working for my brother, Bill, but like I said to him "you'll get plenty of opportunity from many people out there, what you'll do with that opportunity only you can dictate." He's out there doing good right now and as far as Bill told me, his hiring process is in the works.

Putting me in with the youngster also changed the cycle I was on for the first week here. See, they call this (GP) General Population, but it's not. There are three cycles on each unit with 30 inmates on each cycle, and each cycle only receives three and a half hours out-of-cell time per day. The new cycle I became part of (by getting moved to the bottom gallery) placed me in contact with Joseph Fleming, a long-time friend. I actually started my time with his dad and his dad sent word to please watch out for his son before Joseph even got to the prison years ago. Well, Joseph introduced me to his friend, Nicholas Ely, and he had told me the two of them had plans to run a podcast from inside. Immediately a light went off in my head and I asked Joseph if he and Ely wouldn't mind speaking about my case and what the state has done to me so I could finally get it out to the public, the world to see. The next day he tells me Ely is more than ok with doing this and that the state had misused this felony murder law to convict him as well.

I had shown them the two statements that the state had withheld from me, along with the deceptive witness lists and summaries the D.A. had submitted to the court. After a few days I was able to get some laps in on the yard with Ely where I was able to convey my complete history to him and answer any questions he had about this or that. These bumps yet again sent me in another direction, God is awesome! Ely pulled up on me and asked me if I like to write? I said "yeah, I love to read and I am a capable writer, why?" he says he hopes I didn't mind but he had shared my story with his girlfriend during his phone call the previous night and she told him to ask me if I was willing to write out my story in the form of a manuscript. If I was, she'd process it out there into book form and have it printed! Can you believe it? I mean, can you believe it? I can, because God shines through me. He is blessing me. He has used the warden and the administrations mistreatment, knowing their dirty underhanded tactics would place me right where I needed to be for my next bump. I haven't stopped writing since.

I spoke on some of this earlier but I had to ask you to wait for it to come together. On one of my Sunday calls with my brother Bill I was able to share this God given opportunity with him. I told him I had been trying to figure out for some years now how to get my story out into the world and he said to hurry up because he wants to read the completed book. That's when another idea came to mind and I asked if he would please ask Morgan if she'd have the book placed on the internet because Ely had let me know they could provide it to them electronically once it was formatted into book form. We need Morgan so if you're viewing this on the internet? I have to give thanks to her.

Chapter 24

Well, I would just like to thank you for taking your time to read my story. I don't know if I will ever receive the justice this case deserves. I don't know if the crooked D.A. or the North Platte Police Department will ever receive their just due for their illegal unlawful and dirty tactics, but I pray they will be held accountable. No one is above the law, especially those in positions of power that abuse it.

I am really thankful to my Lord and my God for making it possible to have this done, to get this out to the world to see, to read, to question, to demand answers. I'm even thankful for the dirty way in which the people that run NDCS at central office pulled their underhanded brick to place me here. So, stand and be recognized for how you put inmates in these units of segregation without any due process! How you manipulate paperwork to change custody levels and place people in the hole pending made up security threats! MRs are due process, the start of the paper trail, for rule violations. I haven't had an MR in over six years, yet I was placed in segregation without one. I was at the same medium custody level I have been at since 2007 and that is overridden from the community custody level that I qualify for because of my sentence structure. Any custody level change in any direction by policy, has to be justified on paper, yet I just signed a reclass placing me at 1A custody two days ago. "For what reason?" I asked the case manager. She said you have to be 1A to be housed here. I said "I know, but what is the justification for dropping me 3-4 custody levels without any MRs in over six years and no due process being afforded to me?" she said she'd ask but it's what central office said to do. Amazing, isn't it?

I only touched on portions of my time in prison because of my desire is to get my story out to the world. Maybe I'll write a manuscript about my 33 plus years (and counting) in prison in the future. <u>May justice for the lowly finally prevail. God be with you all, thank you for your attention.</u>

≈

Check out other books by More Than an Inmate...

Available now!

Coming soon